Prentice Hall Regents ESL

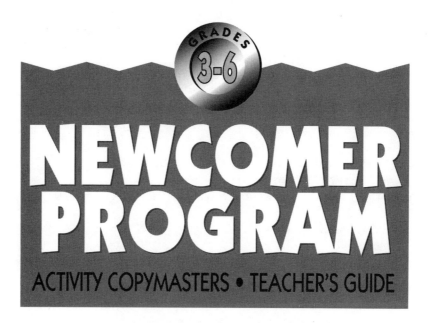

GRADES
3-6

# NEWCOMER PROGRAM

ACTIVITY COPYMASTERS • TEACHER'S GUIDE

## JUDIE HAYNES

## ELIZABETH CLAIRE

## ACKNOWLEDGMENTS

We wish to thank the following professional organizations for providing us with a forum for professional sharing and collaboration:

- TESOL (Teachers of English to Speakers of Other Languages)
- NJ TESOL-BE (New Jersey TESOL-Bilingual Education)
- NJ TESOL-BE Bergen-Passaic Chapter

We also thank our family members for their support while we were working on this project: Judie's mother, Doris Horne, and her husband, Joe; Elizabeth's mother, Anna Eardley, and daughter-in-law, Nadine Simms.

Thanks also to a special group of parent volunteers at the River Edge (NJ) School: Keiko Tanaka, Ikimi Miyake, Tamiko Kiyono, Kyoko Takakura, Kimwha Kim, Mi-Jung Kim, Jung Gyun Oh, Nina Simon, Miyuki Koine, and Yoko Matsumoto.

Publisher: *Marilyn Lindgren*
Development Editors: *Susan Cosentino/Valerie Stewart*
Electronic Production Editors: *Noël Vreeland Carter/Jan Sivertsen/Steven D. Greydanus/Nicole Cypher*
Manufacturing Buyer: *Dave Dickey*
Electronic Image Production Supervisor: *Todd Ware*
Art Director: *Merle Krumper*
Interior Design: *Noël Vreeland Carter/Wanda España/Steven D. Greydanus/Nicole Cypher*
Cover Design: *Wanda España*
Illustrators: *J. D. Frazier/Carey Davies/Steven D. Greydanus/Don Martinetti*

Printed in the United States of America

10   9   8   7   6   5

ISBN   0-13-863036-4

# ❖ CONTENTS ❖

# NEWCOMER ACTIVITY PAGES

## RELATED STORY CARDS*

---

### *KEY TO PHR ESL STORY CARD REFERENCES

Story Cards are an integrated component of the complete PHR ESL Program. They are 16" x 20"
color scenes that provide additional contexts for presenting and using language. Story Cards
are an optional resource; they are not required for the activities in this book.

| Set I | | Set II | | Set III | |
|---|---|---|---|---|---|
| MW | *My World* | WWW | *Water, Water, Water!* | TCE | *Taking Care of the Earth* |
| SMES | *Sun, Moon, Earth, Stars* | EY | *The Environment and You* | ATW | *Around the World* |
| HF | *Having Fun* | AW | *Animal Watch* | SR | *Skeletons to Robots* |
| GC | *Growing and Changing* | AKC | *All Kinds of Celebrations* | MU | *Mysteries and the Unknown* |
| AT | *Around Town* | BE | *Beyond the Earth* | MM | *Marvelous Myths* |
| AA | *Animals, Animals* | M | *Monsters!* | AE | *Adventure and Exploration* |

* See Key at the bottom of page iv.

Related Activities: *Months, p. 43 • Clothing, pp. 49–50 • Things to Do, p. 129*

Related Activities: *Clothing, pp. 49–50 • In the Nurse's Office, pp. 102–106 • Animal Body Parts, p. 157 • Body Measurements, pp. 175–176*

Related Activities: *In Science Class, pp. 107–111*

## MATH

# NEWCOMER PROGRAM

# TEACHER'S GUIDE

This book has been written to help you, your new students, and all future non-English-speaking students who find their way into your class. The materials are designed to help you establish a nurturing environment for the new second-language learners in your classroom and to maximize the learning opportunities for them.

Newcomers between the ages of eight and eleven vary greatly in language, literacy, and academic skills. Students from industrialized nations may be ahead of American peers in some areas and behind in others. Those from poor or war-torn countries may have attended overcrowded schools with few facilities and minimally trained teachers. Some may have not attended much school at all.

Facilitating language learning, social adjustment, and academic development is a challenging task. Support for your newcomers' individualized programs will have to come from a variety of sources. The **Newcomer Program, Grades 3-6** offers an assortment of activity pages and numerous teaching suggestions that address the varied backgrounds and needs of newcomer students.

# USING THE NEWCOMER PROGRAM

The **Newcomer Program, Grades 3-6** provides two essential tools for ESL, bilingual, and mainstream teachers: a comprehensive Teacher's Guide and 176 copymasters of Newcomer Activity Pages.

## TEACHER'S GUIDE

The first part of the Teacher's Guide contains useful information for teachers of beginning-level, limited-English-proficient students. It offers insights into newcomers and their learning styles, and details the emotional, social, and cultural factors that affect the rate at which the new language learners acquire English. There are teaching tips and strategies for mainstream, ESL, bilingual, and special area teachers. Included also is a section on helping newcomers make the transition into content-area work.

The second part of the Teacher's Guide contains the instructions for the activity pages. You will find objectives for each activity as well as multilevel directions and extension activities designed to help you tailor the materials to the needs of your students.

## NEWCOMER ACTIVITY PAGES

This part of the program contains 176 activity pages designed for newcomers in third to sixth grade. They will help students to acquire basic classroom survival skills and a foundation vocabulary for participating in regular classroom instruction. The activities are designed to be flexible. They have been written to require minimal teacher input and can be used independently by the newcomer or given as homework assignments following some initial in-class preparation. They may also be used as instructional interactive activities. It is not necessary to use the pages in the order they are presented in this book. Pages are organized into thematic groups; within a group, there are multiple activities designed to accommodate newcomers of different skill levels. Choose those pages that are appropriate for your newcomer.

The pages are three-hole punched and perforated for your convenience. You may wish to punch holes in the students' copies so that they can keep them organized in a binder.

## RELATED NEWCOMER ACTIVITIES AND STORY CARDS

The table of contents includes cross references to related newcomer activities in this book. There is also a correlation of the newcomer activities to the PHR ESL Story Cards. These 20″ x 16″ illustrated scenes can be used to introduce, reinforce, and expand the language and content of your newcomer program.

# ❖ WORKING WITH NEWCOMERS ❖

*Working with newcomers is an exciting challenge. In this section, you will find a variety of suggestions to help newcomers adjust to their new academic setting and to create numerous and varied learning opportunities. Do not expect to do everything that is mentioned here at once. Get help wherever you can by using the resources around you: buddies, cross-grade tutors, parent volunteers, administrators, ESL and bilingual teachers.*

## PREPARING FOR THE ARRIVAL OF THE NEWCOMER

*Prepare in advance for the arrival of newcomers by setting the stage for a supportive and nurturing classroom environment. Take some time to consider the challenges that the newcomers will face and to anticipate some of the frustrations with language and social adjustment that may arise. The better prepared you are for the new language learner, the more likely he or she will experience a smoother transition.*

**Sensitize mainstream students to newcomers' challenges.** The most crucial needs of the newcomer in the chaos of the new surroundings are not linguistic, but social. Having a good relationship with you and making a friend are the antidotes to many of the painful and frustrating experiences that can overwhelm the newcomer. Whether you are an ESL, bilingual, or mainstream teacher, you realize the need to prepare English-speaking peers to accept and help the new learners of English at recess, in the halls, and on the school bus, as well as in the classroom. When mainstream students accept newcomers into their social networks, they provide them with increased exposure to English and an increased motivation to learn it.

Sensitizing students can be done by the mainstream teacher or the ESL or bilingual teachers. If you are a mainstream teacher, you might wish to call on the ESL specialists at your school for ideas. They may be willing to help you develop classes or conduct consciousness-raising sessions with your students.

Before the newcomer arrives, plan several class periods over a few days or weeks to discuss some of the challenges that confront newcomers. Working with the whole class or in small groups, talk with your students about moving. Share your own experiences of moving and then involve students in the discussion by asking: *Who has moved and changed schools?*

*Who has moved more than once? Where did you move from? How did you feel the first few days? Why? Were things different in your new school? What was different in the new neighborhood? Did you like it right away? How did you make friends?* (Validate the very common experience of feeling like an outsider.) *What did you learn about moving?* If students talk about negative experiences, acknowledge the difficulty involved in moving and build support. Then ask: *What would have helped you feel better about the new school? How could teachers and other students have helped you?*

Be sure to include in the discussion students who have not moved as well. Ask: *Who has always lived here? How do you feel about that? Would you like to move? Why? Why not? Where? What do you think it would be like?*

Next, direct the conversation toward the experience of the newcomer. Have students consider the following questions: *Who would you talk to if no one in your new school spoke English? What would you do to make friends in a new country? When you began to learn to read in the new language, do you think you would be able to read books on your grade level? Would you want to read first-grade books in the beginning? Would you feel bad about reading first-grade books? How would you feel if someone teased you about it?*

Ask bilingual students who have moved to the United States to share some of their feelings. Learning a new language and making friends in a new place is an impressive accomplishment, and these students deserve to be acknowledged for it. Ask: *Who came here from another country? What country? When did you come? Could you speak English? How did you feel? How did you make friends? What helped you learn English? How long did it take? What mistakes did you make? What are the advantages of being bilingual? How many of you can speak another language? Can you teach us to say "hello" in your home language?* Elicit other greetings or words in the students' languages.

**Plan where to seat newcomers.** Think through in advance where you will seat the new student. You may want to seat a newcomer near your desk so you can easily provide help or near a student who has been trained as a buddy. Avoid front-row center and back-row corner seats. Newcomers need a good view of you and the blackboard, as well as of classmates, since they will rely on their cues to learn what is expected and appropriate behavior.

It is also helpful to the newcomer to have peers on all sides with whom to interact. If your class sits in groups, include newcomers with a group of sociable students. Unless you have a specific reason for grouping students of the same home language together, avoid segregating your class by language.

# WHAT IS CULTURE SHOCK?

Culture shock is not just a cliché–our nervous systems really do react biochemically when we are in a strange environment, bombarded with unintelligible noises, unfamiliar faces, and unreadable social signals. Adjusting to a new culture can be difficult for anybody, at any age. Studies among Americans have shown that many adults experience physical and emotional repercussions when relocating to a new town. For as long as a full year, they may be prone to illness, sleep disturbances, irritability, and fatigue. The brain is overloaded with new information to process and make sense of.

Children are even more vulnerable to such changes than adults. The initial shock of being in a strange place without friends or protectors can be quite upsetting. Moving to an environment in which there are not only new cultural expectations but also a new language to learn further increases anxiety. The transition is more difficult for children who are from poor or wartorn areas, who have lived immigration nightmares, or who have been separated from their families. Many of these children now face new economic fears, live in overcrowded, inadequate housing, and suffer discrimination. Since newcomers' parents often do not know what to expect in the new surroundings, they may feel unable to guide and reassure their children. In some cases, parents place additional burdens on their children with unrealistic expectations of immediate academic success.

It is not surprising that many new arrivals have trouble adjusting socially and academically. It is critical both to be aware of the impact that culture shock can have on students and to recognize its symptoms, many of which surface within a few weeks of the newcomer's arrival. Newcomers between the ages of eight and twelve may develop twitches, nervousness, stomachaches, headaches, depression, and hostility. Some children develop defense mechanisms that lead to their being erroneously diagnosed as learning disabled. Some react by withdrawing while others display aggressive and hyperactive behavior. Even students in the upper grades may beg tearfully to spend the day in the shelter of an ESL or bilingual class.

To help counter the effects of culture shock, it is essential to create a welcoming and accepting atmosphere. A good relationship with you and with other students in the class not only will help the newcomers cope with culture shock, but will also ease the transition into their new social and academic environments.

# CREATING A SUPPORTIVE ENVIRONMENT

*Because of the excitement and anxiety that newcomers experience during the first days at school in the United States, their first impression will have a strong impact. What happens in your class will affect the newcomer's confidence, motivation, social adjustment, and even health and attendance. It is critical, therefore, to create a warm and welcoming atmosphere. Such an environment not only contributes to the social adjustment of the child but also allows for more rapid language development and integration into the academic setting.*

❖━━━━━━━━━━━━━━━❖

**Pronounce the newcomer's name correctly.** Your new students have lost so much, don't also let them lose their name. The writing on the student's admission slip may not indicate the correct pronunciation. The staff person who accompanies the child to your door may not have the pronunciation right either. Learn the correct pronunciation of the name from the newcomer (or his or her parents), and practice it until you can say it correctly. It may take a few tries—"Narimsatihar" will not roll off your tongue the way "Benjamin" and "Cassandra" do. Write the newcomer's name on the board with a phonetic version for classmates.

Ask bilingual parents, volunteers, or peers which part of the name is the family name and which is the given name. (Asian names are written and spoken in reverse order from ours; the names may or may not have been reversed in the school office.) Two-part first names are common in many cultures, but to us may appear to be a first name and a middle name. Use both parts of a two-part name. Hispanic family names often consist of two names as well. Ask about them.

Avoid the temptation to Americanize the name or create a nickname for the student. If the student offers a nickname or an Americanized version of the name, however, accept it.

❖━━━━━━━━━━❖

**Help newcomers to pronounce your name.** Write your name on a piece of paper or in the student's notebook. Pronounce it several times for the student, but don't require the newcomer to pronounce it. Introduce the newcomer to at least one other student sitting next to him or her, who will be a buddy. Write down this name for the student as well.

**Make ID cards for newcomers.** Newly arrived students are not yet oriented to the neighborhood and can easily become lost on the way home from school. Write the newcomer's home address, telephone number, and school address on an index card, or use the ID card on page 8. Instruct the student to keep it in a pocket or a backpack. At the end of the first day, make sure that each new student is personally accompanied to the correct bus, or to the place where the parent, sibling, or friend will pick him or her up. If the student walks home, be sure he or she knows where to go and how to get home. Find a buddy who is walking in the same direction.

❖━━━━━━━━━━❖

**Send newcomers on a tour of the school.** If possible, have same-language students take newcomers on a tour of the important places in your school. (Some schools make a video tour for newcomers and their parents.) Reduce the new students' anxiety by teaching them the route to the lunchroom and to the school exit, and back to the classroom. Be sure that newcomers know where the bathrooms are, which one to use (the one marked "Girls" or the one marked "Boys"), what the rules are for leaving the room, and how to ask to go to the bathroom. If no one in your class speaks the newcomer's language, show students where in the building there is a person who *does* speak their home language.

Schools in many countries do not conduct fire drills. Have a bilingual person explain what a fire drill is as soon as the newcomer arrives. The noise from the alarm can be very frightening to a new arrival. (See the activity on page 23, Rules for Fire Drills.)

**Create a personal alphabet.** If your newcomers speak a language that uses a different writing system, tape alphabet cards to their desks so that they will have a model for forming letters correctly. Demonstrate how to write their names using the Roman alphabet, and provide a sample for them to copy. Teach students to write their name and the date on all papers. (See the alphabet activities on pages 29 to 33.)

**Foster social interaction with other students.** Within the first week, foster social interaction by giving your newcomers classroom jobs. Newcomers can help by distributing handouts, collecting homework, and going on short errands with a peer. Allow newcomers to help other class members with nonverbal chores such as patching torn book pages, sharpening pencils, erasing the boards, sorting papers, watering the plants, dusting bookshelves, or any other task that you can demonstrate and that does not require language skills. Acknowledge them for jobs well done.

**Teach survival English right from the start.** Have a volunteer, cross-grade tutor, or mainstream peer help the newcomer to learn and use a few practical phrases and "formulas" needed to communicate basic needs at school. (Make sure not to force students who are not ready for language production to speak. If a newcomer does not seem ready to speak, you will still want to teach survival English, but for recognition purposes.) You might want to suggest that the volunteer or peer begin with phrases for immediate needs, such as "May I go to the bathroom?" After the basics have been covered, have the pair gradually move into language needed to interact with peers, such as "Hello, my name is . . . I'm from . . ." It is also a good idea to have the newcomer practice saying his or her name, address, and telephone number.

You may wish to use the *Welcome to Our School* book on pages 9 to 23 to teach some survival English to newcomers. The high-frequency expressions which are included in these pages will increase the newcomer's ability to communicate in English from the

beginning. Learning these "formulas" expands the language learner's communicative range and boosts self-confidence, allowing even the least fluent students to respond immediately and appropriately in a variety of school and social situations. Have newcomers practice using these phrases in role plays with a buddy.

**Respect the silent period.** Many newcomers between the ages of eight and twelve feel uncomfortable speaking English in an academic setting long after they first arrive. The "silent period" can last anywhere from one day to a year. You may have to explain to students in your class that, even though the newcomer may be speaking a word here and there with them in informal situations and on the playground, he or she may not be ready to produce language in class. Be careful, however, not to underestimate the student's ability to comprehend. A student may not be speaking yet, but that does not mean that he or she cannot function in your classroom.

**Allow frequent breaks from English.** Allow the newcomer time each day during the first few weeks to speak with others of the same home language. It is important that the newcomer be given this opportunity to interact with same-language peers, whether it be to socialize, vent frustrations, or attempt to better understand the goings-on in the classroom.

Encourage the student to write in a home-language diary, read a home-language book, draw pictures, listen (with headphones) to music, or just put his or her head down on the desk and sleep.

**Provide opportunities for newcomers' success.** Don't frustrate your beginning ESL students by asking analytical questions that require a good deal of fluency in English to answer, such as *How? Why? What happened? What's the difference between . . . ?* Newcomers may know an answer but feel unsure of their ability to express it in English. One way to engineer successful participation is to look at newcomers' papers (either homework or in-class assignments) to verify that they have some correct answers. Then call on them to share an answer by writing their response on the chalkboard. Students may feel less threatened by writing answers than by saying them. It also may help to tell students privately in advance that you are going to ask them the question so they can prepare for it.

**Increase wait time.** The typical wait time a teacher allows after a question in a mainstream class discussion is 5 seconds. A newcomer may know the answer but need 15 to 20 seconds to formulate it in English. One way to allow newcomers more wait time and thereby encourage their participation is to ask a question that has a number of possible answers and refrain from calling on anyone while you erase the blackboard, wipe your glasses, or clear your desk. If they volunteer, call first on newcomers, who will have had time to compose an answer. If a newcomer gives a wrong answer, acknowledge it as a good try and reword the question as an either/or choice. Comments such as "Good guess," "Almost," or "Thank you for trying," will encourage students to continue participating when they have answered incorrectly.

Write out this list of responses for your newcomers and have students practice using them.

❖ "I don't understand the question."
❖ "I understand the question, but I don't know the answer."
❖ "I know the answer, but I can't say it."
❖ "Please wait."
❖ "Please repeat the question."

**Use cooperative learning strategies.** Inclusion in cooperative groups provides newcomers with a powerful incentive for learning English. The beginning language learners benefit from listening to and sharing with their peers. Although much of the English will be above their level of comprehension, they will be able to participate at some level in many of the activities. Mainstream students also benefit from the inclusion of newcomers in cooperative groups. After working with them in this setting, mainstream students often become more accepting of culturally different students.

Select themes that come from your students' interests and needs, and that draw together literature, hands-on activities, songs, poetry, chants, games, and group projects. If the class is studying fairy tales, for example, newcomers can show a version of a popular fairy tale from their own culture. They can also help work within the group to act out the fairy tale or draw pictures for a report.

**Teach students to use a bilingual dictionary.** Every ESL student, beginning in the third grade, should have a bilingual dictionary appropriate to his or her grade level. If parents can't provide dictionaries, ask the library or media center to order them in the languages of your newcomers so that each student can borrow a dictionary for the year. If the students don't know how to use a dictionary, ask parents or bilingual volunteers to teach them. Allow beginning students to use their dictionaries freely to verify new vocabulary.

**Rely on personal observation for assessment.** Don't rely on school records to assess newcomers. It is often difficult to determine whether or not a newcomer has grade-level academic skills in his or her home language. In some cases, there are no past school records and/or transcripts. (Some newcomers may have never gone to school or may have missed several years of schooling.) If transcripts are available, they are likely to be in the home language. Even if records have been translated, the educational standards may be quite different from ours. You may have to rely on your observations and your experience as a teacher to assess the newcomer's academic skills. Keep in mind that your initial assessment of academic competence is likely to undergo changes as the newcomer develops more language ability and becomes more comfortable in your classroom.

# NEWCOMERS' FRUSTRATIONS

*Newcomers have a lot of adjustments to make as they learn to survive in the school culture. This is no easy feat, as it involves figuring out what is being asked of them, determining which behaviors are considered acceptable by the group, and negotiating social contacts across language and culture barriers. Below are excerpts from ESL students' essays, offering a glimpse at the personal struggles they have endured. (Some quotes have been translated from the home language.)*

- My parents wanted to come here, but I didn't. I miss my home, my grandparents, my dog, my friends, my school team, and all the things I love. There is no one here I can count on. English makes my head hurt.

- When students laugh, I think they are laughing at me. I feel as though I don't belong here.

- I was very happy to come to America, and there are a lot of things I like. The teachers are very kind. But I have no friends to play with or talk to about my feelings. Many days I spend the lunch time all by myself. I can hardly swallow my food then.

- The teachers keep saying "Speak English" when I talk to my friend. But I don't know the words I need to say, and my friend wouldn't understand me if I spoke English.

- American kids yell "Speak English!" at me, too. They get mad because my friends and I speak our language at recess. If we laugh, they think we're laughing at them, and they start a fight with us.

- I would like to do something to show my teachers that I can learn, but they give me work that is too hard. Then they think I'm lazy because I don't do it.

- Sometimes I don't know what the teacher wants me to do, but she is busy and I am afraid to ask her. It is very boring.

- I study very hard at home, but I don't want to answer questions in class. Someone always laughs at my mistakes. I can't understand the questions on the tests, so I can't show what I know. On the report card, the teacher gave me "U" for effort. My parents got very angry and punished me.

- Someone talks on the loudspeaker every morning, and I never know what they are saying. Then later I find out that I was supposed to do something, like sign up for baseball, and it's too late.

- In my language, every letter has only one sound. You just write what it sounds like. I do that in English and nothing is right.

*Often, newcomers do not communicate their frustrations to a classroom teacher because they don't have the language to speak to the teacher, or because they blame themselves for the problem. With the help of bilingual personnel, volunteers, or older students, encourage newcomers to speak about their feelings. The positive relationship that can result from such interaction may help to foster social and academic development as well.*

# USING BUDDIES TO HELP NEWCOMERS LEARN

*A classroom teacher does not have the time to provide all of the instruction needed by ESL newcomers. You can, however, increase the avenues through which the new second-language learners acquire English by using students as peer teachers. Peer teachers not only multiply your efforts but also provide age-level social support. In addition, the experience of being a "deputy teacher" may be one of the most powerful learning experiences English-speaking students have in their school career. Remember to provide buddies with orientation, training, on-going guidance, and acknowledgment for the very special contributions they make.*

**Assign bilingual buddies.** A buddy who speaks the newcomer's language is a wonderful asset, particularly immediately following the newcomer's arrival. During the adjustment phase, the peer buddy can help ease the newcomer into his or her new environment. Peer interaction of this sort is a great self-esteem builder for the bilingual buddy and provides the newcomer with a friend.

You may want to rotate buddies so that students do not become too dependent on one person and the bilingual buddy does not miss too much work. An imposed companionship of same-language speakers for longer than a few weeks may actually hinder both students: a same-language buddy who feels burdened by continually helping newcomers may become resentful and the newcomer may come to rely on having work translated rather than trying to construct meaning on his or her own.

**Use English-only buddies, too.** In addition to helping newcomers with the activity pages from this book, English-speaking buddies can help to make newcomers feel welcome by assisting them with work and having fun together. Ask students to brainstorm ways they can do this. After students have offered some ideas, suggest a few additional examples.

❖ Sit with newcomers at lunch time.
❖ Help them with their homework.
❖ Learn how to communicate with them using gestures and short phrases.
❖ Read to newcomers, or listen to taped books with them.
❖ Walk home with them, or sit with them on the bus.
❖ Teach them the alphabet, numbers, rhymes, and beginning vocabulary.
❖ Include them in games.

❖ Learn a song or greeting in the newcomer's first language.
❖ Record stories or other material for them to listen to. (See page T30 for additional ideas on having buddies make audio tapes for newcomers.)

**Provide buddies with tips.** Teach buddies the importance of being patient, repeating, and not overwhelming newcomers. Show them how to help without doing the work for the newcomers. Encourage them to use gestures, mime, pictures, and props to provide clues to meaning as they speak. Help them understand that some newcomers might feel too shy to speak for several months after arriving but that buddies should continue to speak and socialize with the new language learners.

Reward students who take their job seriously. Contributing to the newcomers' education will provide a real and immediate purpose for improving the buddies' own reading, writing, spelling, speaking, listening, teaching, patience, and other life skills. When asked to help a newcomer learn, academic underachievers sometimes gain a new sense of self-esteem and motivation. Keep in mind, though, that newcomers should be paired with a variety of classmates for a wide range of social contacts and potential friendships.

**Use cross-grade tutors.** In addition to same-age buddies, you may want to try cross-grade tutors. Older bilingual students in particular can be very helpful to recently arrived newcomers of the same home language. The cross-grade buddies can explain classroom procedure and rules to the newcomers as well as help them with the newcomer activity pages. Be careful that tutors do not miss too much of their own work.

# ORGANIZING MATERIALS FOR LANGUAGE LEARNERS

*Find a shelf, a closet, and/or a large box to keep materials and equipment for your language learners. Label everything in this language learning area and organize it so that students, buddies, tutors, and volunteers can easily find what they need. Be sure to indicate where each item belongs so that students can return material and equipment to the correct places.*

*Each day, you may want to indicate in writing what materials you want newcomers to work on. Use page numbers, draw pictures, or have a bilingual student or volunteer translate to communicate what work you want done. Students will feel more comfortable if they know what is expected of them and if they have specific goals to meet.*

**Gather materials and supplies for the language learning area.** Listed below are some of the items you may want to include in the language learning area.

❖ a folder for each student containing copies of appropriate newcomer activity pages from this book

❖ a box to store file folders for newcomer activity pages

❖ a commercial and/or a class-made picture file

❖ a picture dictionary

❖ picture books and beginning-to-read books

❖ texts that have been written especially for ESL students in the content areas (Choose books that have lots of illustrations and that use controlled vocabulary and sentence structures.)

❖ nonfiction picture books from the school library that illustrate content you are currently teaching in your science, social studies, or health classes

❖ ESL versions of classics

❖ home-language texts in science, social studies, health, etc.

❖ home-language story and literature books at the appropriate reading level

❖ well-illustrated magazines for browsing and cutting

❖ a tape recorder and earphones

❖ cassettes of student- or teacher-taped material: the *Welcome to Our School* book (pages 9–23), the *New People in My Life* book (pages 24–28), the alphabet, the Pledge of Allegiance (page 134), picture dictionaries, songs, stories, textbooks, etc.

❖ taped readings of well-illustrated beginning-to-read books

❖ phonics books with tapes

❖ taped music in both English and home languages (Whenever possible, supply the written text of the songs.)

❖ flash cards: alphabet flash cards, vocabulary/picture flash cards, blank flash cards or index cards

❖ a box containing small objects and manipulatives for vocabulary or phonics teaching

❖ materials for making and storing instructional aids: blank index cards, file folders, markers, glue, tape, shoe boxes

❖ games: concentration games, word bingo, Scrabble™, Boggle™ cubes, word searches, alphabet dot-to-dot activities, and jigsaw puzzles that contain type, maps, and cultural scenes

❖ student-made materials

❖ a computer with CD-ROM voice capacity and basic software including word identification programs, spelling programs, simple reading and math programs, and language games

# PROVIDING PRODUCTIVE WORK
# FOR NEWCOMERS

*The more comfortable they are in your classroom and the greater their self-esteem, the more ready to learn your newcomers will be. Conversely, the more anxiety students experience, the less progress they will make in language development. Provide materials and create situations that will help students gain confidence in their language abilities. Like other students, newcomers need daily opportunities for success. Challenge students at an appropriate level, but be careful not to call on them to perform alone above their level of competence.*

*This section presents ideas for providing newcomers with meaningful and challenging tasks in English and content-area work at a variety of language levels. At first, independent activities may be the largest component of the newcomers' day. They will have a voracious appetite for work that is on their level, and the activity pages in this book will help to get them started. Introduce newcomers to the materials in the language learning area (see page T11) in your room, and allow them time to work with items in the box, either independently or with a peer tutor or parent volunteer. Make sure to provide clear instructions for what you expect newcomers to do.*

**Make up individualized packets of materials for your newcomers.** Until the newcomer is able to participate in class activities, he or she will need individualized materials to work on. Prepare a packet of activity pages for each newcomer. Select appropriate pages from this book and add any other materials that are relevant to each newcomer. Choose activities that can be easily explained. Have students work on material from their individualized packets when they cannot follow the work being done in the classroom. Add to the packets periodically, as newcomers complete the work and as classroom subject matter changes.

**Assign and monitor appropriate copy work.** One of the first things newcomers can be productively engaged in is copy work. Assign copy work on an individual basis to match a student's abilities and to develop a needed skill. For example, students whose home languages do not use the Roman alphabet will benefit from copying:

❖ individual letters.

❖ their own names and others' names.

❖ the names of objects in the classroom (which have been labeled by classmates).

❖ words from a picture dictionary.

Provide students with a sans serif model of the letters or words on lined paper so they can write directly below the models. (Beginning students who have been assigned copy work from a textbook [or serif model] may meticulously copy all the hooks on a serif typeface.)

Literate students whose first language uses the Roman alphabet (or students who have learned to write the letters of the Roman alphabet) benefit from a different type of copy work. Assign copy work from material that is both familiar and comprehensible to newcomers. This might include:

❖ stories that have been read to them.

❖ captions from their content textbooks.

❖ a paragraph from a content textbook.

Copying exercises help to develop fine motor skills, letter formation, left-to-right progression, vocabulary, spelling, word order, punctuation, sentence structure familiarity, and content-area knowledge. Remember, however, if the student doesn't first know the sounds and meanings of the words he or she is copying, the activity becomes busywork. Avoid extensive copy work sessions, as students' hands may cramp from writing too much.

**Establish good work habits.** Newcomers need to learn that they are accountable for the productive use of their time even when they are not involved with the class lessons. Helping them to develop good work habits and to be self-directed will take some time, but it is well worth the investment. Give newcomers regular and appropriate assignments. Be specific and clear in your directions, and write them down for students. If your instructions are vague, some students will do nothing. Others will struggle to complete the assignment as given to the rest of the class. Check to be sure that students understand what they are to do, particularly during the first several weeks as student work habits are being established. Demonstrate standards of neatness and form, and make clear the amount of time you expect students to spend working. When newcomers have begun to internalize these standards, you can delegate routine explanations and corrections of assignments and activity pages to buddies, paraprofessionals, or volunteers.

**Use rote learning.** Although not popular in American schools, rote learning skills are highly developed in many countries. In addition, parents and students often feel more comfortable if they can see an end product. Don't limit newcomers' learning to rote memorization, but if it comes easily to your students, capitalize on their ability to learn in this manner.

Have students use a picture dictionary to make self-checking study sheets of words they want to learn. Demonstrate how to fold a paper lengthwise, write the vocabulary words in the left column, and home-language translations in the right column. Show students how to cover the right column and test themselves on the meanings of the vocabulary words. Then demonstrate how to reverse the process by covering the words in the left column and trying to recall and/or spell the English words.

**Compile a picture file.** Invite all of your ESL, bilingual, or mainstream students to bring in old magazines. List categories of pictures to look for—animals, clothes, food, actions, places, and occupations—and have a group "bee" activity. Ask students to cut out pictures, select the most useful, and then mount them on 9″ x 12″ index cards or oak tag. Have students neatly write the words or sentences for the pictures on the back. Sort the pictures into categories, and store them in a cardboard box.

Have newcomers work in pairs to first learn the words and then create sentences or stories suggested by the pictures. Or have the newcomers work alone, using the cards to test themselves. Suggest that they copy the words (or sentences) into a notebook. Encourage buddies to informally test the newcomers on vocabulary or spelling.

**Make vocabulary posters in cooperative groups.** Have each group of students create a large poster of a category of common vocabulary words. Categories might include food, clothing, body parts, colors, animals, playground scenes, the family, classroom objects, street scenes, house and furniture, or transportation. Have students cut out pictures from magazines and then glue them to large sheets of construction paper or poster board. After students label the posters, display them around your classroom.

**Make concentration card games.** Have newcomers create sets of concentration card games using the vocabulary cards (pages 43, 49–50, 56–57, 64, 69, 155–157, and 161) from this book. Use 3″ x 5″ index cards and cut them in half. Tell the students to glue the pictures from the vocabulary cards on one side and the words on the other side. Each game should have between eleven and fifteen pairs.

Encourage students to help newcomers make more personalized concentration card games as well. Ask them to choose a category—i.e., numbers, colors, animals, fruits, vegetables, clothing, toys, body parts, or transportation—and make a list of easy-to-illustrate words they will use for the cards. Check their spelling. Have them draw a picture on one card and clearly print the matching word on another card. Suggest that they test their pictures on classmates to ensure that the picture is identifiable. When students play the games, they should say the name of the picture out loud to help the newcomer acquire the targeted vocabulary words.

**Provide plenty of aural input.** Beginning-level limited-English-proficient students need to be continually exposed to the sounds of the English language. Whenever possible, read activity pages and other materials to your newcomers. Enlist the aid of buddies, cross-grade tutors, paraprofessionals, and volunteers to help you in this effort.

Use a variety of sources for this aural input, including commercially-produced and/or teacher- and student-made audio tapes. A recording multiplies your efforts and also allows the students to listen to the tape as many times as necessary. Supply a comfortable set of headphones so that students may listen without disturbing the rest of the class. The recordings should be at a slow-to-normal pace, with sufficient pause at the end of each sentence to allow students time to mentally connect the picture, text, and sounds of the language. Show newcomers how to use the pause button on the cassette player. Label all recordings completely, and keep them in appropriate containers. A word of caution, however. The student using headphones is isolated from the rest of the class. Limit the use of headphones to reasonable sessions.

**Focus attention on accomplishments.** Focus your feedback on newcomers' efforts and accomplishments rather than calling attention to errors. Give lots of encouragement and praise for what the students can do. If newcomers appear apathetic, fearful, or frustrated, have them take a deep breath, do some stretches, or go for a walk to the water fountain. When possible, allow students to choose from several activities.

**Use newcomers' strong modes of learning: visual and kinesthetic.** It is unrealistic to expect students to sit for long periods of time, listening to language that is above their level of comprehension. Of the auditory, visual, and kinesthetic learning styles, newcomers will find auditory the least useful. Capitalize on their ability to learn and understand through visual and kinesthetic modes. Try to make the content of your lessons comprehensible, even to the least proficient students, through illustrations, dramatic gestures, drawings, actions, blackboard sketches, photos, demonstrations, and other visual support. Kinesthetic movements and hands-on activities also help to make language more comprehensible to newcomers. Visual and kinesthetic support is beneficial not only to your ESL students but will help all learners in you class.

Dedicate a few minutes to your planning each day to decide what visual aids, dramatizations, reenactments, or hands-on aids will help in getting the messages across. Collect resources and tools for making language comprehensible to students. Share your ideas and materials with grade-level colleagues.

**Reinforce language learning with written support.** Write key words neatly on the board, read them aloud, and define them with pictures. Allow newcomers time to look up the words in their bilingual dictionaries. Matching spoken words to print will help to reinforce the key vocabulary from your oral lessons. It also enables your students to practice linking oral and written language.

**Provide a variety of activities for newcomers.** Set limits on the amount of time students listen to tapes or work on the computer. Vary a day's assignments to include work from more than one subject area. Involve newcomers in different types of activities and tasks—copy work, guided writing, coloring, drawing, tracing, cutting and pasting, matching, rote memorization, map work, puzzles, research, home-language reading and writing, as well as interactive tasks, group work, and hands-on activities—that develop all four language skills.

# QUESTION STRATEGIES FOR NEWCOMERS

*When formulated to match his or her language level, questions will provide you with feedback on a newcomer's understanding. Questions that are too challenging linguistically are frustrating to the students and will not provide you with an accurate idea of the student's level of comprehension. Ask the question that best allows the newcomer to demonstrate comprehension of material and ability to communicate. Students' participation correlates closely to their success rate. If a newcomer responds successfully to a majority of questions, he or she is likely to continue participating. Conversely, if a student is consistently unable to answer questions, he or she will lose both confidence and interest. Following is a hierarchy of question types listed from simple to more complex.*

❖ Ask the newcomer to point to items in a picture, words on the blackboard, or locations on a map. If he or she does not understand the directions or the vocabulary, have another student demonstrate the answer. Then repeat the question, using the same words.

❖ Using visual cues, ask simple yes/no questions. (Example: Holding the classroom scene from page 71, ask *Is Miss Rose teaching math?*)

❖ Ask either/or questions in which the answers are embedded. (Example: *Is Miss Rose teaching math or science?*)

❖ Break complex questions into several steps. For example, rather than asking *What are the people in the picture doing?* try breaking the question into a few small manageable parts.

> TEACHER Look at the picture. (Pause.) Point to Alain. (Student points.) Good. What is he doing?

If there is no answer, rephrase the question with a choice of answers.

> TEACHER Is Alain writing on the chalkboard or reading a book?

With the correct answer embedded in the question, the student need only recognize, rather than recall, the language needed.

> STUDENT Writing.

> TEACHER That's right. Alain is writing on the chalkboard.

❖ Ask simple *who, what,* and *where* questions that can be answered in one or two words. Students must go beyond recognition to recall and formulate a response in English.

❖ Ask *how* and *why* questions that elicit short-sentence answers. Encourage students to express themselves.

*Watch students' body language for signs that they want to participate. A student may know an answer but be afraid to respond and hesitantly raise his or her hand only a few inches. Be sure to encourage students to speak and allow them sufficient time to formulate a response.*

*Do not require that ESL students put their oral responses into complete sentences. This reduces their ability to participate. Accept one-word answers. If you wish, supply the complete sentence in your acknowledgment.*

# DEVELOPING PRIDE IN THE NEWCOMER'S HOME LANGUAGE AND CULTURE

*It is important to encourage newcomers to maintain and value their home languages and cultures. In addition to helping your newcomers develop a sense of pride in who they are, you are helping them to build schemata, skills, and strategies that will eventually transfer into English. Include assignments in your classroom that relate to each newcomer's home country, language, literature, flag, customs, and life experiences. The material becomes more meaningful to the newcomers, and the class benefits from exposure to new cultures and languages.*

**Help newcomers value their language and culture.** When you ask newcomers to share their home language and culture, you are helping to build their self-esteem as well as their confidence in your classroom.

❖ Have newcomers add home-language words to English labels, or make new labels, for classroom items. Then invite them to teach their words for classroom items.

❖ Post pictures drawn by the newcomers that reflect the geography, climate, culture, dress, animals, vegetation, food, farms, buildings, transportation, customs, flag, etc. in their home countries.

❖ Post maps of your newcomers' countries and have each student locate and highlight his or her town or city.

❖ Invite newcomers to write home-language greetings in large letters using markers. Hang the greetings. (If the language uses a non-Roman alphabet, include a phonetic equivalent.) Ask newcomers to teach the greetings to classmates, working with small groups.

❖ Have newcomers demonstrate the formation of letters or characters in their writing system.

❖ Show the class a movie or film strip about the newcomers' native countries. Have the students participate in setting up the VCR and "presenting" the shows.

❖ At holiday time, invite students to teach holiday songs in their home languages or demonstrate games and customs from the holidays.

❖ Have the newcomers bring in home-language books, newspapers, or magazines. Give English speakers in your class a chance to understand the challenge of learning to read in a new language. The newcomers will enjoy "teaching" their classmates.

❖ Have newcomers make home-language audio tapes of stories they are familiar with or have read. Then invite them to illustrate the stories.

Build and encourage interest in other languages. Tell students that you will add their name to the language learner's honor roll if, for example, they learn to count to ten in a new language. You might also invite bilingual parent volunteers to teach your class a game or song, or simply share some other aspect of their home culture.

**Tap the newcomer as a resource.** The newcomer brings to the classroom a wealth of cultural knowledge. Tap into this knowledge and encourage students to learn information first-hand from the newcomer. Assign social studies information-gathering projects in areas being studied in class.

❖ Geography *Where is the country that Alain comes from? How far away is it? What continent is it on? What kinds of work do people do there? What is the climate like? What kinds of houses do people live in? What kind of clothes do they wear? What animals and birds live there? What languages do people speak there? What is the capital? Who is the leader?*

❖ Language *Listen to Po Wen and his sister speak. What do you notice about the sounds? Can you guess what they are talking about?*

❖ Cultural customs *Why does Usha's mother have a red dot on her forehead? Why does Kentaro use sticks to eat with? Why does Yusuke wear short pants when it is cold out? Why does Youssef's mother wear a scarf tied around her head?*

❖ Religious customs *Why doesn't Osvaldo pledge allegiance to the flag when the rest of us do? Why doesn't Shammi eat any food at all on certain days?*

You may want to monitor these question-and-answer sessions to make sure that students discuss cultural differences in a respectful and open manner.

Invite newcomers to demonstrate a culture-related skill or to bring in hobby items. In small groups or one-on-one settings, have them teach mainstream students:

❖ a simple song or nursery rhyme.

❖ a playground game or a jump-rope chant.

❖ the equivalent of "eenie meenie miney mo" for choosing leaders or teams.

❖ origami.

❖ the use of chopsticks.

❖ hand-clapping or finger games.

❖ string games, such as cat's cradle.

❖ customs (i.e., bowing, using two hands to hand things to people).

❖ stories, folktales, heroes.

# AMERICAN SCHOOLS THROUGH THE NEWCOMER'S EYES

*Cultural differences can account for many of the misinterpretations and misunderstandings that occur when we are working with newcomers. If a student's behavior seems unwarranted, bizarre, rude, or in some way unexpected, it is possible that this is a sign of cultural difference rather than disrespect. The newcomer may be behaving exactly as he or she should, given his or her cultural values and norms. Schools in many countries are more autocratic than in the United States. Teachers may be stricter, lessons more formal, and rules more rigid. Corporal punishment is common in many countries. Students learn by rote, may stand when reciting, and are sometimes punished for errors and failures. Whether they fear or love teachers, students are taught to show a high degree of respect. We might think that newcomers would be glad to find themselves in a more relaxed atmosphere, but what is relaxed by our standards may seem chaotic to newcomers.*

*Awareness on your part will help reduce cultural misunderstandings in your classroom. Seek information from bicultural personnel or parents, or from books and in-service workshops that discuss the different cultures of your students. The following reactions from second-language learners are offered here to help teachers better understand their newcomers' behavior.*

## PEDAGOGICAL APPROACH

Most newcomers will not have experienced education as individualized learning, group projects, and partnerships. Students and their parents may misinterpret American methods and the teachers' informality as lax discipline and inferior education.

- Teachers sometimes say, "I don't know." Science experiments don't always turn out. Some students point out teachers' mistakes and disagree with them. (Can these be good teachers or respectful students?)

- Teachers expect students to learn by talking together in a group. (Is this real work? Teachers are older and wiser, and they, not students, know the answers.)

- Teachers ask students to express personal opinions or debate and argue different sides of a question. (Teachers are supposed to tell us the answers. I want the teacher's opinion, not other students' opinions; students are not wise.)

## PHYSICAL CONTACT AND SENSE OF PERSONAL SPACE

Americans are comfortable with an arm's length of distance between them and non-intimate others. Students from some cultures prefer to be closer while those from other cultures prefer to stand farther away. Depending on the country of origin of the student, Americans may seem either distant and cold or pushy and overly familiar.

- The teacher and other students crowd in too close. When I back away, they keep coming at me.

- The teacher and other students keep backing away from me.

- Teachers hug, kiss, and squeeze young students. (Don't touch me please. I'm not a baby.)

- The teachers never hug us. (Don't they like us?)

- Teachers pat students on the head, and students play keep-away with my hat. (The head is the most sacred part of my body, and no one is allowed to touch it.)

## GENDER ROLES

In many countries, gender roles are rigidly defined and students are often separated by gender.

- Boys and girls are in the same classroom. They sit next to each other, and even attend gym classes together.
- There are family life discussions with both boys and girls at the same time. (I would never tell my feelings about such things in front of boys/girls.)
- Textbooks show men doing women's work and women doing men's work.
- There are mostly women teachers and even a woman principal.
- Women are not gentle and quiet and respectful to men in this school. Men do not do all the hard jobs, but let women do some of them.

## SCHOOL ATTIRE

Many students around the world must follow a school dress code. The freedom to dress as one wishes in most American schools is surprising to many newcomers.

- Students don't have to wear uniforms. They wear whatever they want—expensive clothes or ragged jeans. They may wear their hair any length. Girls may wear earrings and makeup. Fashion seems important. And expensive. (Are my clothes funny? Should I get my ears pierced?)
- Girls wear pants to school. Even women teachers wear pants.
- Everyone wears their outside shoes inside the school, instead of special slippers.

## SCHEDULES, ROUTINES, AND RITUALS

The schedules, routines, and rituals of the American school culture may be very different from those in other countries. Newcomers may not understand many of these customs at first.

- There is no school-wide assembly or exercise class in the morning. The principal doesn't make a speech to us every day about doing our best work.
- Students change class for music, art, gym, computer, and other subjects. I have six different teachers.
- The teacher doesn't eat lunch with us. (The teacher is supposed to be with the students all day.)
- American students ride to school in a bus or their parents drive them to school.
- There is heat in the school hallways. (How can they waste fuel this way?)

- Students wear long pants, sweaters, and heavy jackets. (How can they make their bodies strong?)
- There are no breaks each hour to play or talk. It's not clear when I can go to the bathroom.
- Americans smile at you even when they don't want to be friends. (This doesn't seem sincere.)
- Americans say a prayer to the flag every morning. The teacher wants me to learn it too, even though I have my own religion.
- The teacher leans or sits on the edge of her desk. (Why doesn't she have respect for the most sacred place in the classroom?)
- Teachers and students use one hand instead of both hands when they give things to people and accept things from a superior.
- Students and teachers sometimes hand things to people with the left hand. (This is such an insult in my country!)

## INDEPENDENCE AND INDIVIDUALISM

In the United States, independence and individualism are valued and promoted both at school and in society at large. Some newcomers arrive from cultures that value group harmony and cooperation above all else and reject independence and individualism as self-serving.

- Students raise their hands to get more attention for themselves. Teachers don't make sure each person gets an equal chance to speak. Teachers have favorites.
- American students like to argue. They don't try to create group harmony or make sure others have a turn and are respected.
- Americans are independent and expect other people to be independent, too. They are not very sensitive to others' feelings.

## CRIME AND VIOLENCE IN SCHOOLS

The phenomena of crime and violence in schools is new, and quite frightening, to many of the second-language learners who arrive in this country.

- Some students steal things. Some students carry weapons to school. It's dangerous to be in the halls, stairways, and streets.
- Older students or gangs steal from, and hurt, younger children and those who walk alone. Will I be safe?
- Some students use drugs and act stupid or crazy.

## TEACHER RESPECT

In many countries, teacher and student boundaries are very clearly defined, with the teacher being accorded the respect given to a sage.

- American students boldly call the teacher by her name. She doesn't like it when I use the respectful title of "Teacher."
- Some students talk during class or disobey the teacher. Sometimes the teacher gets really angry and yells at the students and punishes everyone. It's frightening.
- Students speak to the teacher without waiting for the teacher to call on them. (I would be afraid to do this; the teacher is very busy.)

## HYGIENE AND FOOD

Every culture has its own standards of hygiene. Newcomers may find that some of the American standards run counter to those they are familiar with.

- Americans smell funny.
- Americans say I smell funny.
- People eat food with their hands and lick their fingers. They eat when walking down the street.
- Americans kill and eat animals; they drink milk and eat eggs; the school cafeteria serves taboo foods.
- Americans blow their noses in public, and even at meals!
- Sometimes the teacher licks her thumb to separate the papers before she gives them to students.

## GOOD THINGS ABOUT AMERICAN SCHOOLS

There are, however, some aspects of American schools that newcomers enjoy.

- School is free.
- Books are free and have beautiful pictures.
- There are desks and chairs for everyone.
- There are no air raid drills.
- There are windows in the classroom.
- There's no sound of gunfire.
- It's all right to be my religion.
- The teachers are kind. I won't be beaten.

# TEACHING NEWCOMERS TO READ

*There are many factors to consider when teaching newcomers to read. Are the students already literate in their home language? If they are literate, does their home language use the Roman alphabet, or a different alphabet? If different, does that writing system read from left to right, from right to left, or from top to bottom? If students are not literate in their own language, is that because they haven't attended school yet, or because they did not succeed with the instruction they have had so far? Do you have a single ESL student in your class, or half a dozen? What are the ages of your students? Does your school system embrace the whole language philosophy for reading, or are you using a phonics-based traditional approach? Do you use a basal reader, authentic literature, or a combination in your reading instruction?*

*Because of the variables to consider when teaching newcomers to read, you will need to individualize your teaching approach to each student's unique literacy profile. In this section, you'll find strategies for a wide variety of situations. Choose those that fit your student's age, ability level, and needs. Regardless of the approach you take, remember that second-language learners who are in a socially supportive environment and use language in meaningful ways will have more motivation for learning to read in English. Strive to create an environment in which students learn all language skills, including reading and writing, in a natural way and for real purposes.*

**Read to newcomers every day.** Reading comprehensible material to your students and engaging them in appropriate extension activities are effective ways to introduce students to English print and the pleasures of reading. Enhance your readings with pictures, gestures, and dramatic intonation to convey meaning. Don't worry if students don't understand every word. It is more important that they have general comprehension of the whole story or text. Reading meaningful texts to newcomers helps them to build vocabulary and to develop confidence in their ability to comprehend. It also familiarizes them with the sound system, grammatical patterns, and rhythms of English. Students find reading sessions nonthreatening and pleasurable. You may want to delegate some of the oral reading instruction to a volunteer, peer, or cross-grade tutor.

Appropriate reading material for beginning ESL learners should include at least some of these characteristics.

❖ numerous illustrations that help clarify the text

❖ story plots that are action-based

❖ little text on each page

❖ text that contains repetitive, predictable phrases

❖ high-frequency vocabulary and useful words

❖ text that employs simple sentence structures

Enlist the aid of kindergarten and first-grade teachers, the librarian, and the person in charge of the media center to locate and select suitable literature.

**Use reading strategies to increase students' comprehension.** When you read to beginning ESL students, be sure to make language comprehensible to them.

❖ Point to the corresponding pictures as you read the text.

❖ Act out, dramatize, and provide models and manipulatives for students to handle.

❖ Read sentences at a slow-to-normal speed, using an expressive tone.

❖ Allow time after each sentence or paragraph for students to assimilate the material.

❖ Verify comprehension of the story by asking students to point to items in the illustrations and to answer yes/no and either/or questions.

❖ Read the same story on successive days. Pause at strategic points and invite students to supply the words or phrases they know.

- ❖ Point to the words in the text as you read them. This is particularly useful for students who need to learn the left-to-right flow of English text.

- ❖ When students are familiar with the story, invite them to "read" along with you as you point to the words.

- ❖ If appropriate for younger students, use Big Books, as both text and illustrations can be easily seen. (However, if you are a mainstream teacher, you might not want to use Big Books for any of the newcomers. The books may appear babyish and embarrass the language learners.)

**Teach the alphabet.** Preliterate students and literate third- to sixth-grade newcomers who speak a language that does not use the Roman alphabet need direct instruction in letter recognition and formation as well as beginning phonics. See pages 29 to 33 for beginning alphabet exercises. If you wish to give your students more practice with letter formation and sound-symbol correspondence, you may want to use first-grade mainstream materials. Students who have already developed the concept of sound-symbol correspondence in their own language will have a much easier time learning to read in English.

**Use authentic literature.** While useful in some respects, basal readers present a number of problems for the newcomer. To begin with, they are not written with ESL students' needs in mind. While they present no difficulty to English speakers, passive sentences, subordinated ideas, and idiomatic expressions greatly hinder a newcomer's comprehension. Words selected for decoding purposes may be low-frequency vocabulary items and therefore not useful to the newcomer. Moreover, a first-grade basal reader will not appeal to a fourth- or fifth-grade student, and its juvenile appearance can be embarrassing.

Carefully selected authentic literature from your school library or from a lower-grade classroom is better suited to the needs of newcomers. Materials that are especially prepared for ESL students, with controlled sentence length and high-frequency vocabulary, are also good choices. If you do use a basal reader with your ESL students, be flexible. Select stories that have easily understood action plots and skip those with plots based on feelings, abstractions, or plays on words.

**Teach phonics in context.** Using authentic literature, you can introduce and reinforce letter recognition, beginning and ending sounds, blends, rhyming words, silent letters, homonyms, etc. Phonics worksheets are not generally useful to the newcomer since they present new vocabulary items out of context. In addition, the lack of aural input does not allow the new student to make sound-symbol correspondences. The inconsistencies in English phonics are confusing to the second-language learner, and rules learned in isolation are less likely to be applied than phonics taught in the context of a pleasing story. If you feel you need to use phonics worksheets, provide taped audio input so students can learn the pronunciation of letters and words as they work independently.

**Make sure students understand the meaning.** Your students may learn to decode accurately but be unable to construct meaning out of the words they have read. Sometimes students know the meanings of the individual words in a sentence or phrase but lack the grammatical awareness to understand the relationship among the words. "The dog was eaten by a snake" may seem identical to "The dog has eaten a snake." Teach newcomers to reflect on what they have decoded and to ask questions to be sure they understand.

**Check comprehension through sequencing activities.** Check student comprehension with one or more of the following activities. Write individual sentences from the text on separate sheets of drawing paper; then read or have the students read each sentence and illustrate it. Informally test students' ability to sequence material from a story: print sentences from a section of the story on paper strips; mix the strips; have students work together, or with a buddy, to put them in order. Check students'

ability to order words within a sentence: write several sentences from the text on individual strips of paper; cut the strips into words; have students arrange each group of words into a sentence.

**Provide for audio review.** Set up a tape recorder and record stories as you read. Newcomers then have the opportunity to listen to a story, and read along, as many times as they wish. Texts, such as the paragraphs describing the school and community scenes in this book (see pages 72, 79, 84, 88, 92, 98, 103, 108, 113, 118, and 122), can be taped by mainstream students or volunteers. See page T30 for additional ideas on involving mainstream students in making audio tapes.

**Use environmental print.** ESL learners are eager to read the print that surrounds them in the classroom and in the community: *Exit, Push, Boys, Office, Burger King, ShopRite, Exxon, Stop, No Parking.* Take advantage of student interest by sending newcomers around the school to collect samples of environmental print. As a homework assignment, ask them to compile a list of environmental print from within the community: store names, building or street signs, and text from packages. Use environmental print as a springboard for developing whole-class lessons on topics such as health, safety, nutrition, etc.

**Involve newcomers in Sustained Silent Reading.** Provide time for SSR (Sustained Silent Reading) and allow students to select books they enjoy. Offer a selection of easy-to-read books and comic books.

**Teach reading in the home language first.** Whenever feasible, students should have an opportunity to receive reading instruction in their home language prior to receiving reading instruction in English. If there is no bilingual program at your school, and reading instruction in the home language cannot be arranged through the school or parents or community, preliterate students should receive developmental reading instruction. Both the reading teacher and the ESL teacher are qualified to give such instruction. It is best to provide individual instruction or to group the student with other preliterate students of the same age. Note that this reading instruction should be in addition to the students' time in ESL class. If you are a mainstream teacher and find yourself responsible for the developmental reading instruction of preliterate newcomers, allow newcomers time to develop some aural familiarity with English and build a vocabulary base before beginning reading instruction.

**Encourage reading outside of the classroom.** Stock your classroom library and language learning area (or box) with plenty of picture books, easy-to-read books, magazines, and comic books. Encourage newcomers' parents to join the public library and check out picture books, books with read-along tapes, and home-language books, if available. Ask parents to read to their children in their home language and, if they can, in English.

# ANTICIPATING CHALLENGES IN LEARNING TO READ ENGLISH

*There are many challenges in learning to read English. Some students will not know how to read from left to right. Others will have different names for the letters of the alphabet and will associate them with different sounds. Still others will have learned to construct meaning directly from written characters, as we get meaning from a picture, and will not be familiar with the concept of sound-symbol correspondence. Being aware of such challenges will help you to better tailor reading instruction to each newcomer.*

**Sound-symbol correspondence can be problematic for the newcomer.** If your students are literate in a Roman alphabet language, they will associate different sounds with many of the letters in the English alphabet. This will interfere with oral reading as well as with spelling. The English language contains forty-four sounds, but has only twenty-six letters to represent those sounds. This means that a large percentage of English words contains an exception to phonetic rules, making it particularly frustrating to learn to decode and spell in English. For students who speak languages that have a one-to-one phonetic correspondence between sound and symbol, such as Spanish and Polish, distinguishing homonyms and studying spelling are unfamiliar concepts.

**Home-language sentence structure can interfere with comprehension.** The more that the grammar of their first language differs from English, the more difficult it is for newcomers to comprehend what they are reading. Swedish speakers have few problems learning to read English because the grammatical patterns of the two languages are quite similar. Speakers of Asian languages, on the other hand, are greatly frustrated by the seemingly backward word order and strange inflections of English.

Typical word order in English—subject/verb, or subject/verb/object—is not universal. In Spanish, for example, the subject is often omitted, as it may be understood from the verb ending. In Japanese, the word order is (subject) object/verb, with the subject, more often than not, omitted. English has prepositions while many Asian languages have *postpositions*.

Dependent clauses, participles, passive forms, two-word verbs, compound tenses, and sequence of tenses, among other things, present problems for those who speak languages that do not have these types of grammatical structures.

**Lack of cognates increases difficulty.** The fewer the cognates in the home language and in English, the more difficulty the newcomer will experience with American vocabulary. Hungarian, Chinese, and Vietnamese, for example, do not share many words with English. Students speaking these languages will have to learn a greater number of English vocabulary items than students whose first language shares a large common vocabulary base with English, such as Dutch. The Japanese have borrowed many American words for Western clothing, food, and imported items, but since there are no cognates in basic vocabulary areas, Japanese students also face a wide vocabulary gap.

**Learning to read from left to right takes time.** Arabic and Hebrew students who read from right to left will feel as if they are reading backwards. It will take time to accustom the eye muscles to the reverse process, reading from left to right. Word reversals such as *saw* for *was* will be common for a while. These students will also need a great deal of practice in producing legible handwriting.

**Do not overwhelm preliterate newcomers with reading instruction.** Preliterate newcomers need at least some oral competency before they can benefit from reading instruction in

English. For students in grades 3 through 6, not knowing how to read may produce great frustration and low self-esteem. Teaching letter recognition or phonics before students are familiar with the sounds and meanings that correspond with the symbols you are asking them to interpret, proves frustrating for teacher and student alike. Read to and converse with your preliterate newcomers daily, and continually work to expand their aural language base.

The following steps outline a basic strategy for teaching preliterate upper-grade students to learn to read in English. Keep in mind the social stigma these students are likely to feel about their lack of previous schooling, and help enhance their self-esteem by acknowledging each successful step, no matter how small. Proceed as slowly as necessary. Build confidence one step at a time, evaluate and review, and follow the student's lead. If a student seems overwhelmed, return to an earlier step.

1. Teach the names of the letters of the alphabet. Have newcomers practice daily by listening to a tape and pointing to the letters they hear.

2. Teach the words *same* and *different. (These are the same: 0/0. These are different: 0/8.)* Once students have mastered these concepts, assign exercises that help them distinguish between the shapes and sounds of letters. *(These letters are the same: p/p. These letters are different: p/d.)*

3. Provide exercises in moving a pencil along lines from left to right.

4. Teach students to recognize, say, and write the letters in their names. Add other letters as each group of letters is mastered. One letter a day can be enough; don't rush. As soon as you teach the name of a letter, present it in the context of a known word, such as a classmate's name or a key word in a familiar story.

5. Use as many modes for learning as possible: point out letters in the words from stories you read; have students hunt for letters around the room; have students cut out letters or make clay letters or form letters from toothpicks; etc.

6. Have students explore surrounding print and common vocabulary such as students' names, labels around the room, textbook and subject names, environmental print, names of favorite foods and possessions.

7. During independent work time, students can:

❖ identify letters in words.

❖ find and circle every occurrence of a certain letter in a short paragraph.

❖ make alphabet flash cards, of both upper- and lowercase letters.

❖ trace letters.

❖ manipulate and sort letter blocks.

❖ copy letters and words.

❖ make illustrated booklets of words that begin with the sound of each letter, with the help of a picture dictionary.

❖ listen to well-illustrated, taped stories and follow along as the text is read.

**English words may be confusing to newcomers.** The English language contains thousands of words that function differently depending on the context within which they appear.

❖ **Multiple meanings** Words with multiple meanings can cause misreadings. The newcomer may not differentiate "We went to a play" from "We went to play." The same is true with words that can be more than one part of speech, such as *light. (Light* the *light* blue *light* so it will be *light* in here.)

❖ **Idiomatic expressions** There are thousands of idiomatic expressions in English, many of which are problematic to the new reader. Often a reader knows the meaning of individual words, but can't distinguish when a group of those words forms an idiom. For example, a newcomer who knows the words *cut, out,* and *that,* will not know that "Cut that out" means "Stop what you're doing, it bothers me."

❖ **Prepositions and articles** Even good readers will be tripped up by prepositions and the articles *a, an,* and *the.* "He has *a few* friends. She has *few* friends." (Who has more friends?)

# CULTURAL CONSIDERATIONS IN READING

*Even when the student knows the meaning of the individual words in a story, under-stands the relationship of the words and sentences, and can recite the story from memory, comprehension is not fully guaranteed. In order to comprehend the author's message, a reader must be aware not only of what the author has said but also of what has been left unsaid. ESL learners who seem to read quite well and may even state that they understand a story often miss the real point because they do not share the cultural background needed to properly interpret the story.*

**Background information is not universal.** There are endless themes, characters, issues, expectations, and norms in American children's literature that will differ from those that the newcomer brings with him or her. Story elements which we assume to be universal can be problematic for the language learner. As he or she reads, the ESL student struggles to make sense of the information that lies outside the realm of his or her cultural back-ground. For example, all American chil-dren know that dogs are pets and that the relationship between a dog and its owner is often one of affection and loyalty. Therefore, we see no need to explain such a relationship when it appears in a story. The newcomer whose culture does not regard dogs and cats as pets, however, may not understand the underlying premise of a story based on the friendship of a boy and his dog.

Similarly, American children know that mice (in stories) are cute and dolphins are intelligent; they know what the tooth fairy is up to, and that catching frogs in the summer is fun, that baby sitters are a fact of life, and that girls as well as boys can climb trees and play ball. They also know what good and bad manners are, and have growing stores of references for holiday customs, folk heroes, and myths. Also within the American child's cultural back-ground are birthday parties, lemonade stands, allowances, tree houses, clubs, scouts, summer camp, slumber parties, Little League, playgrounds, and circuses. The six o'clock news and other TV fare have exposed American students to topics such as sex, violence, gay rights, sexual harassment, racial discrimination, drugs, pollution, government corruption, and AIDS; these topics have woven them-selves into the fabric of the student's cultural background. English-speaking students are also familiar with the convention of portraying dolls and stuffed animals as characters. They have been exposed to friendly ghosts, witches, and monsters. They have been raised on story themes that include the notions of independence, individuality, sibling rivalry, rebelling against authority, desire for recognition, overlapping gender roles, and material versus emotional and psychological rewards.

Many of these conventions and themes, however, are likely to be new to the newcomer, and some may even be in direct contradiction to the student's own values and expectations. Story themes and premises, like jokes, may not translate, and endings to stories may be inexplicable and unsatisfying to newcomers, even though they understand the individual sentences.

**Bridge the cultural gaps in reading.** In the early stages of reading instruction, choose stories that are within the scope of the learner's background. This may include classic folktales, literature from the student's home country, and stories dictated by the learner. Drawing on experiences and norms that are within a student's cultural background will enable the

new language learner to fully participate in a reading. Although the actual words and sentence structure may appear to be at the same level of difficulty as those in other materials you use, these stories will be much easier for newcomers to comprehend.

When you begin to introduce stories that include themes based on U.S. culture, help newcomers build new cultural schemata, or background knowledge. Use prereading activities to provide students with an understanding of the culture-related key words and assumptions. For example, before reading a story about a boy and his dog, introduce newcomers to the concept of pets. Discuss the types of animals that we usually keep as pets, whether or not they or classmates have pets, and general features of the pet-owner relationship.

**Consider the degree of cultural distance.** The degree of cultural distance influences reading comprehension. ESL learners from industrialized Western countries will share more cultural similarities with Americans, and may comprehend what they read more readily than Asians, rural Central Americans, or Africans, who are at a greater cultural distance from the texts of American authors.

# WRITING IN A NEW LANGUAGE

*Students learn to write more effectively when they have real reasons to communicate. Create situations in which they need to write invitations, requests, thank you notes, letters to pen pals, cards for special occasions, morning news and weather reports, commercials, and opinions. Have them conduct surveys (pages 45–46, 55, 60–61, and 149), write reports based on the surveys, and then post them for the class to read. Many of the activities that you do with your mainstream, bilingual, or ESL students can be adapted for newcomers.*

*Until students can express themselves in written English, encourage journal and letter writing in the home language. Acknowledge the value and accomplishment of each student's writing, even if you cannot read it.*

---

**Instruct students in the proper formation of letters.** Give students not familiar with the Roman alphabet plenty of extra writing practice. As you demonstrate the proper formation of letters, teach the name and sounds of each letter. Have students practice the formation of each letter using lined paper that is appropriate to their grade and ability level. Teach students only as many letters at a time that they can handle. You can find handwriting exercises on pages 29 to 33. If you wish to give your students more practice with letter formation, you may want to look at second- or third-grade mainstream handwriting materials. The text in these books will be more comprehensible to most newcomers than a grade-level textbook.

Students whose native writing systems progress from right to left need particular patience. Set standards of legibility, neatness, and attractiveness for all writing, but keep in mind the difficulty of relearning to write using a new alphabet.

Before assigning copy work from readers or textbooks, remember to check that students know how to form letters. Newcomers who are unfamiliar with the Roman alphabet may painstakingly copy all the serifs on each letter. Provide a handwriting copy book or daily worksheets. Make sure students know the meaning of what they are copying.

---

**Teach cursive writing to newcomers.** If you teach the upper elementary grades, you will often write in cursive on the chalkboard and on materials you prepare for the class. While you may ask an English-speaking classmate to read cursive text aloud to newcomers at first, it is important to help newcomers in grades 3 through 6 learn to read and write cursive script as soon as possible. (You will want to teach cursive after newcomers have learned to read and write printed text.) Provide ample practice; the ability to write in cursive is a demonstrable accomplishment that builds self-esteem. You will find examples of cursive writing and a practice template on pages 32 and 33. (Newcomers who are not familiar with the Roman alphabet are learning four new sets of symbols: upper- and lowercase block and cursive letters. Pace your teaching so as not to overwhelm them.)

---

**Individualize writing activities.** Providing newcomers with meaningful reasons to write increases their levels of interest and motivation.

❖ Have students create language books and label the pictures. Staple sheets of construction paper together and have students cut pictures out of magazines to make booklets to show personal likes and dislikes (the "I Like" book); abilities and lack of abilities (the "I Can" book); or categories of items (The Food Book, The Animal Book, Tools, Machines, People, Occupations, Toys, and Places). Have students use their bilingual dictionaries to label the pictures.

❖ Have students make their own books by drawing or cutting out pictures and then writing captions and word balloons.

❖ Encourage newcomers to keep a daily journal of ideas or quotes from classmates.

**Use students' lives as writing topics.** Ask students questions about their lives and families, likes and dislikes, hobbies, etc. Write their answers; then have the newcomers read them to you. Have them illustrate their answers to make books and then practice reading each other's stories.

**Teach writing as an extension of reading.** Writing is closely related to reading and cannot be taught in a vacuum. Students learn to read and write when they are engaged in reading and writing for meaningful purposes, not by filling in blanks in workbooks, nor by doing pages of isolated phonics drills. Here are some beginning writing activities that build on the reading experience.

After students read a story:

❖ Invite them to illustrate the story and write appropriate captions or word balloons. Accept invented spellings, thereby encouraging the creative thinking/writing process. (If the product is to be displayed or reproduced for others to read, supply a word bank for each student to use in proofreading spellings or encourage students to double-check the spelling in the story.)

❖ Have students dictate the story in their own words to an English speaker. Encourage newcomers to watch as the partner writes. Help them to read back their own words and share their story with others.

❖ Have students tell and then write their own variation of the story. Encourage imagination, incorporation of additional characters (or themselves) into the story, narration of the story in a different time (the past or future), turning the tables (having the bad guy really have a good heart), etc. This activity can be completed in either English or the first language.

❖ Create hands-on activities that support a theme from the story. Write out the steps in that activity. For example, after reading "The Three Bears" you might suggest that students (1) make instant oatmeal, (2) set the table, (3) serve and eat the oatmeal, (4) talk about the oatmeal (*It's hot/cold/delicious/sweet,* etc.), and (5) clean up. Write a group story about the activity.

❖ Have students make simple comparisons of characters and situations. Read different versions of the same story and ask students to identify the similarities and differences. Write student responses on a chart.

# INTEGRATING NEWCOMERS INTO THE MAINSTREAM CLASSROOM

*Language learning is a social phenomenon; the more newcomers interact with their mainstream peers, the more motivated they will be to learn English. Within the first week, foster social interaction by giving your newcomers classroom jobs. Mainstream students are a valuable language resource for newcomers and can help to ease their transition to the new school environment. Have your class brainstorm ways to involve newcomers in academic activities and to help them learn English.*

**Create a social context for learning.** Newcomers who work in cooperative groups have real reasons to learn English. They are an essential part of the class community and have a contribution to make. Have groups brainstorm what tasks their non-English-speaking members can be involved in (helping with illustrations, charts, maps, measurements, calculations, folders, covers, labels, etc.). Assign the second-language learners roles that are integral to the success of the project, ensuring interaction with the other students in the group. Hold the group responsible for the newcomers' learning by setting concrete learning objectives—that the newcomer be able to identify places on a map, answer one simple question, or state two key sentences, for example.

**Have mainstream students make audio tapes.** Teach your mainstream students how to make audio tapes for your new learners of English. Demonstrate how to speak at a slow but natural pace, using a lot of expression. Have your mainstream students make tapes of the *Welcome to Our School* (pages 9–23) and *New People in My Life* books (pages 24–28). For the former, you may have one person record the entire script or you may assign one student to each of the six different roles. To personalize the *New People in My Life* script, you might have each person read the two sentences that he or she has written. Additional materials that mainstream students can record for the English-language learners include:

❖ items that are labeled around the room. (You may want to number the objects so that they can be referred to on tape by number.)

❖ the Pledge of Allegiance. (See page 134.)

❖ the Alphabet Song.

❖ the numbers from one to twenty, by tens to 100, by hundreds to 1,000. (See pages 36 and 37.)

❖ the parts of the body. (See pages 146 and 147.)

❖ the text for the school and community scenes. (See pages 72, 79, 84, 88, 92, 98, 103, 108, 113, 118, and 122.)

❖ the words in a children's picture dictionary. (Number the pictures so that students can follow the tape.)

**Be generous with thanks and praise.** Be sure to frequently acknowledge the contributions of your mainstream students and to point out the progress made by the ESL students they have helped. Reward the whole class when your newcomers make progress. Thanks and praise will go a long way with cross-grade tutors and bilingual parent volunteers as well. Let all those who help know that you appreciate their efforts.

**Involve newcomers in mainstream thematic activities.** Thematic units unify language arts, writing, science, social studies, and math. If you use a thematic approach with your mainstream students, you can involve your newcomers from the very beginning. They will not understand a lot but will be able to participate on some level. Following are some examples of thematic activities that a third- to sixth-grade teacher might use in a unit on food and nutrition. Most provide excellent opportunities for ESL students, even those with very limited

English, both to develop language and to learn grade-level concepts. The culminating activity is a class luncheon.

Begin the unit by having a class discussion about students' current eating habits and preferences. You may want to prepare newcomers by working with them on several of the activity pages on food (pages 56–61) in this book. Read the teacher's instructions for additional ideas. Then have students:

❖ Read stories that revolve around food, followed by a science chapter or magazine article on nutrition. Involve the newcomer by selecting simplified materials at his or her reading level.

❖ Bring in food packaging labels, such as cereal boxes, to read and discuss.

❖ In cooperative groups, calculate the calories and percentages of fat in a school lunch menu.

❖ Conduct blindfolded taste tests of different cereals. Help newcomers expand their vocabulary to include *crunchy, crispy, mushy, sweet, dry*, etc.

❖ Do tongue-mapping for bitter, sour, sweet, and salty sensations.

❖ Watch and report on TV food commercials. Simplify the newcomer's task and ask him or her, for example, to name the food items presented.

❖ Read about the diets of athletes. Newcomers might draw pictures or look up (in a bilingual dictionary) words from a list of the food items in an athlete's diet.

❖ Decide how to differentiate junk food from nutritious food.

❖ Create commercials for nutritious foods. Involve the newcomer by having him or her draw the foods being advertised and then label them.

❖ Design a bulletin board display on nutrition. Newcomers can cut out pictures of foods and place them in the appropriate spots on a food pyramid.

For the class luncheon, have mainstream students and newcomers work together to:

❖ Plan a nutritious lunch.

❖ Make a budget and then write up a shopping list.

❖ Collect and count money.

❖ Take a class trip to the supermarket and compare costs of economy- and single-size packages.

❖ Write luncheon invitations to the principal, school nurse, etc.

❖ Purchase all the items needed for the luncheon; wash, peel, and cut the foods; prepare, serve, and eat the lunch they have planned.

❖ Clean up and recycle the recyclables.

❖ Write their impressions of the luncheon in a daily journal. (If they cannot yet write in English, newcomers can draw and label pictures of food that was served.)

To review what students have learned in the unit on food and nutrition, have them create a class newspaper or book about food and nutrition, including news stories, opinion or advice columns, research reports, recipes, book reviews, puzzles, photos, illustrations, and cartoons. Newcomers can contribute illustrations, copy captions or labels, help position items on pages, glue items in place, or make covers.

# TEACHING CONTENT-AREA SUBJECTS

*If you are a mainstream teacher or teach an integrated curriculum, you will want to ease newcomers into the content areas one subject at a time. Because math is a universal system based on visual symbols, many teachers include students in this subject first. However, if the student is below grade level in math, you may want to consider science as the first subject area in which to make newcomers responsible for participation and work. Science is a good choice because it can be made very visual and concrete, with hands-on learning opportunities; most students like it, and it does not require previous mastery of earlier concepts the way math does.*

*Allow for success in one subject area to occur before inviting the student to tackle more. (The lower the grade level, the sooner additional subject responsibilities can be added.) Ask students how many hours of homework they are doing before you challenge them with more responsibilities. Many ambitious students will spend three to six hours after school struggling, with dictionaries and parents, to translate texts. Help them by giving them reasonable goals and appropriate responsibilities.*

*Regardless of the content area, capitalize on the newcomers' strengths. If students have a preference for rote memorization, do not deny them this method of learning. (Make sure that the material students are memorizing is comprehensible to them.) It is more logical for them to memorize the states and their capitals than it is to make sense of a history chapter when their reading skills in English are still undeveloped. The recognition gained from demonstrating what they have learned helps to build self-esteem, and the rote-learned information will not go to waste. Use your students' abilities in art as well to involve them in making maps, charts, and pictures.*

## ❖ MATH ❖

*The English of math lessons can usually be made visually comprehensible to ESL learners. Students who have grade-level math skills will not only have an opportunity to display their competence but will also pick up a great deal of English during math presentations. If a student is not on grade level in math, enlist the help of a parent or bilingual volunteer to teach and drill computation in the home language. The following are suggestions for integrating newcomers into your regular math instruction.*

### NUMBER VOCABULARY

To learn the sounds of the English words for numbers, have students work with an English-speaking buddy, volunteer, or cross-grade tutor. They may begin with the activities on pages 36 and 37 and then continue working independently with tapes.

### MATH TERMS

Help newcomers learn key words that indicate each of the different math operations. Teach basic shape, line, and measurement words as well. Pages 171 to 176 offer an introduction to some basic measurement and geometry terminology.

### MONEY

Our coins are confusing to newcomers. The values are not numerically indicated on the coins, and the smallest coin in the American monetary system (dime) is twice the value of a larger coin (nickel). Provide coins for newcomers to work with. (Model coins can be made by mounting coin illustrations from page 166.) Have a student ask the newcomer for various amounts of money. Set up a store, using realia or pictures. Assign prices to each item. Have students take turns asking about prices, purchasing items, and making change. Use pages 169 and 170 to get students started. (See pages 166 to 170 for exercises with money.)

### TIME

Time can also present problems for newcomers. If you have ever traveled abroad and tried to figure out what time your plane was leaving (16:25), you can understand the reason for confusion. See pages 39 and 40 for exercises with time. Have students make a daily schedule (page 70), indicating the times that they have different classes and subjects.

## PUNCTUATION

Point out to students from South American and European countries that we use a comma to separate thousands while they use a period. (Their *4.000* is our *4,000*.) Also point out that we use a period as our decimal mark while they use a comma. (They write *3,4* while we write *3.4*.) Help students learn how to read large numbers and pronounce decimals and fractions.

## METRIC SYSTEM

Most of the world uses the metric system. Math concepts based on feet, inches, miles, pounds, ounces, cups, pints, quarts, etc., are best learned through hands-on activities. Have newcomers measure their books, their desks, pens and pencils, the classroom, windows, and the blackboard with rulers and tape

measures. Have them weigh books, themselves, classmates, and various objects in the classroom. Provide containers for them to measure liquids. Have them write up their findings in chart or graph form. See pages 174 to 176 for activities on linear measurement.

## FAHRENHEIT

Familiarize newcomers with Fahrenheit temperature readings by having them keep a chart of outdoor temperatures during the month. (Hang a thermometer outside your classroom window.) See pages 139 to 145 for this and other temperature-related activities.

## WORD PROBLEMS

Math word problems often present difficulty for second-language learners. Illustrate word problems by showing (or drawing) pictures and indicating the number operations. Allow the use of bilingual dictionaries. If you assign ten word problems to the class, assign only one, two, or three to the newcomers.

---

### ❖ CULTURAL DIFFERENCES IN MATH INSTRUCTION ❖

*There are many cultural differences in math instruction around the world. Awareness of these differences will help you to anticipate and resolve your newcomers' confusion with American conventions in math operations.*

❖ The order in which math skills are taught varies from country to country. Computational skills such as multiplication and long division are taught earlier in some countries than in the United States whereas geometry concepts, such as shapes, angles, parallel lines, perimeter, and area, may be taught much later. In many cultures, math is taught by rote in the earlier grades. A third-grade newcomer may be able to do long division but will possibly not know many of the basic math concepts included in third-grade curriculum in the United States.

❖ The mechanics of performing operations in some cultures differ from those taught in the United States. Students from South America and the Caribbean may display their work for division problems in a form quite different from that seen in the United States.

Example: 4,756 divided by 41

$$
\begin{array}{r}
116 \\
41\overline{)4756} \\
\underline{41}\phantom{56} \\
65\phantom{6} \\
\underline{41}\phantom{6} \\
246 \\
\underline{246} \\
0
\end{array}
$$

U.S.

Haiti  $\dfrac{4756\,|\,41}{116}$

❖ In many countries, students learn to do math computations in their heads and don't show their work. Newcomers may be quite frustrated to have to learn a less efficient way of computing numbers. If they consistently get the right answer, let them continue with their method of computing.

# ❖ SCIENCE ❖

*Science has more cognates in other languages than social studies, language arts, or reading. Words like* pollution, electricity, animal, plant, mammal, vertebrate, cell, microscope, system, skeleton, vision, *and many other science terms have easily recognized cognates in Romance and Germanic languages. In addition, science textbooks help to make concepts comprehensible by offering many opportunities for demonstrations and hands-on activities. Such activities not only help newcomers to comprehend language but also cultivate student interest in science.*

## SCIENCE DEMONSTRATIONS

When conducting a science demonstration, teach the names of the materials and apparatus you are using. Give a descriptive narration during the demonstration. (Example: *Now Jay is connecting the wire to the battery. He is turning the switch. Did the light go on?*)

## TRANSITIONAL ASSIGNMENTS

First assignments in science can include copying or drawing diagrams, charts, and graphs; making dioramas and models; and helping with demonstrations. Have students work on projects in groups.

## CLASS EXPERIMENTS

Create experiments for all of your students to talk, write, and think about. For example, have students observe the feeding behavior of hermit crabs in a class terrarium. Newcomers might draw a picture of the crab and label its features (*shell, claws, antennae, eyes,* etc.). Or you might suggest that they draw and label all the things a hermit crab can do (*crawl, eat, drink, fight, climb, pinch, change houses,* etc.). Have newcomers write short sentences and assemble an illustrated book. They can also describe the materials, procedure, and results on a lab report form with help.

# ❖ SOCIAL STUDIES ❖

*Newcomers usually arrive with more catching up to do in social studies than in any other subject. Social studies discussions and texts assume years of background knowledge about the United States. Newcomers may know as little about the United States as American students know about the history, geography, and national heroes of the newcomers' native lands. You might have newcomers work independently on carefully selected social studies assignments to help them learn some of the basic concepts and vocabulary being taught in the social studies curriculum.*

## BASIC TOPICS

If possible, ask the media specialist for a list of well-illustrated books on a beginning-to-read level that introduce students to North American heroes, holidays, and history. The books should contain only a few lines of text per page. Help students keep a record of the books they read.

## AURAL INPUT

Have an English-speaking buddy, cross-grade tutor, or volunteer read some of the books to the ESL student. Having the English speaker record some of the stories on tape will allow for additional aural practice.

## PICTURES THAT TEACH

Provide books that will teach through pictures, even if the text is too difficult for newcomers. Paging through a picture dictionary stimulates interest in many topics. Trade books done in photo-journalistic style are also good.

## HOME-LANGUAGE TEXTBOOKS

If there are many students of a particular language in your school, enlist the help of your colleagues—the bilingual teacher, ESL teacher, and media specialist—to locate elementary level social studies texts in the newcomers' language. Many materials are available in Spanish, and there is a growing number in Asian languages. (Depending on the country of origin, the perspectives and coverage may differ from an American point of view.)

## GRADE-LEVEL CONCEPTS

In the language learning area (see page T11), include simplified texts that introduce grade-level concepts in each of the content areas. Some publishers specialize in this type of book. Check to see if the media center can order a few. You might also have newcomers use the regular classroom textbook, but assign short, manageable sections and provide in-class preparation.

# ❖ SPELLING AND VOCABULARY ❖

*ESL learners acquire vocabulary and learn spelling best through extensive reading for academic purposes and for pleasure, just as native speakers of English do. (Keep in mind that reading for pleasure may be a new concept for children from some cultures, who are accustomed to reading only when studying.) In addition to reading, second-language learners develop a vocabulary base through purposeful writing tasks. Students learn most quickly those words that they need for meaningful communication.*

## INVENTED SPELLING

Allowing for invented spelling enables students to tap their creative thinking processes when writing. If you insist on correct spelling at this stage of writing, students will become overly concerned with form, and content will suffer. When you review the paper, you might provide a word bank with the proper spellings at the bottom of the page. Have students correct the misspelled words using the word bank.

## PERSONALIZED SPELLING LISTS

Encourage students to create lists of spelling words from their own reading and writing. Show them how to study the words by saying the letters aloud several times and then copying them. Have students test one another in pairs. Remember to check that students understand the meanings of the words they memorize.

## TRADITIONAL SPELLING EXERCISES

If traditional spelling word exercises and spelling tests are part of your curriculum, you can incorporate newcomers from the beginning. Adjust the number of words they are responsible for on spelling tests, selecting those words that can be demonstrated or illustrated, or add five words especially chosen for the new language learners to the class list. Words from a picture dictionary work well since students will know the meanings of the words they are asked to spell. Don't be afraid to have students learn words by rote or by copying words ten times each. This may be more effective than using spelling workbooks, which are complicated for newcomers and require a great deal of teacher input and explanation.

## VOCABULARY IN CONTEXT

Teaching new words from vocabulary lists is not usually effective. The out-of-context words are meaningless to newcomers, and vocabulary included in definitions and sample sentences is often too difficult for the new language learner. Vocabulary is learned best in context, when reading meaningful texts and stories. If every new word had to be learned individually, out of context, there would not be enough time to learn the tens of thousands of words needed to succeed in school.

## VOCABULARY ACTIVITIES

Have the student work with new words in a variety of meaningful ways. You might have students:

- ❖ listen to someone pronounce the words.
- ❖ alphabetize the words.
- ❖ find the words in a bilingual dictionary and write the home-language definitions.
- ❖ draw pictures of those words that can be illustrated.
- ❖ write an English synonym for each word.
- ❖ listen to a buddy use the words in sentences that illustrate the meanings.
- ❖ say and write sentences to demonstrate knowledge of the words.
- ❖ make a word search puzzle containing the new words.

# MODIFYING ASSIGNMENTS IN GRADE-LEVEL TEXTBOOKS

*Newcomers will need modification and tailoring of regular classroom assignments for a long time. However, the type of assignment that works for entry-level students in September is no longer an appropriate challenge in December. Following are suggestions for gradually integrating textbooks into the newcomer's academic responsibilities.*

❖ Have students look at the visuals in the chapter and think about what they see in the pictures. Reassure them not to worry about reading the text at this point.

❖ Ask students to copy the chapter title, subtitles, and captions.

❖ Have students copy a chart, make a graph, or draw a picture, time line, table, or diagram.

❖ Have students trace a map, and then label the individual parts of the map (i.e., cities, states, rivers, mountains).

❖ Invite English-speaking students to record part of a chapter on tape. Have newcomers read along and listen to the sounds of English.

❖ Pair the new language learner with a buddy. Tell the buddy to talk about the pictures in the chapter and to read the captions aloud to the newcomer, pointing out key vocabulary that you have selected.

❖ Write a list of key words from a chapter for the students to find in their bilingual dictionaries.

❖ Have students write about what they understand or see in the pictures. Allow them to write in their home language if they can't do it in English, or have them use a bilingual dictionary to locate and write the English words.

❖ Choose an illustrated paragraph or column that is significant in the chapter. Ask a buddy to read the segment aloud to the newcomer, or have someone record it. Have students read the material three or four times, look up new words, and write the words and their meanings in a notebook. Then have students copy the selection. Tell the buddy to ask yes/no questions and questions requiring a one-word answer.

❖ Teach students to skim a chapter to find answers to questions. Show them how to direct their focus by previewing the questions before they read the chapter. Have them copy the sentence or paragraph that contains the answer to a question.

# FACILITATING PARENT-TEACHER CONFERENCES

*Parents of non-English speaking students are anxious about their child's success at school. Often, they harbor unrealistic expectations and place additional burdens on the newcomer. Before discussing their child's performance at school, let parents know your expectations for second-language learners. Help them understand that language learning is a long process and that acquiring grade-level academic skills will take a number of years.*

*When you meet with parents, emphasize the student's language development and growth in learning. The standard school report card doesn't fully communicate the scope of the newcomer's language, academic, and social progress. Offer as many comments and anecdotes as you can about the student's accomplishments. Keep comments simple and easy to understand. Describe what the student does in class. Acknowledge effort and willingness to take risks. Show samples of the student's best work. Remember that each newcomer's situation is unique, and with so many variables there is no reliable standard of comparison with peers or students of previous years.*

*Before discussing any problems that the child is having, consider your comments carefully. Parents may mistakenly feel that their child has shamed the family and deserves to be severely punished. Try not to make vague comments. Could do better, for example, provides parents with no useful information. Let parents know what you and the school are doing to improve the situation, and suggest ways they can work with you to help the child.*

❖━━━━━━━━━━━━━━❖

**Use newcomers' portfolios.** Use portfolios to show parents a student's progress. Show the student's writing samples, drawings, test papers, etc. In parent-teacher conferences, visuals provide the most effective means for communicating a student's effort and growth at school. Even if the parent brings an interpreter, the portfolio enables you to communicate directly. Allow parents to take a copy of the portfolio home.

Avoid using number or letter grades, if possible. They do not provide the type of feedback that will be helpful to most parents. However, if your school gives modified grades to ESL students, be sure that parents realize when a grade is modified.

❖━━━━━━━━━━❖

**Use various modes of communication.** Use the same strategies for communicating to parents that you use with your ESL students. Invite parents to ask questions or indicate if you are speaking too quickly. Provide both visual and aural input. Write out statements that might be misinterpreted. Convey your availability and willingness to help through facial expressions, body language, and tone of voice.

Keep in mind that cultural differences may interfere with communication. For example, parents who nod their heads and say, "Yes, yes," to your suggestions and comments may not mean "Yes, I agree," but rather "Yes, I hear you."

❖━━━━━━━━━━❖

**Affirm the newcomer's home language and culture.** Increase the parent's respect for their child and their own culture. Let parents know that students of different countries can learn a lot from each other. Mention a specific incident or example that illustrates how their child's home language or culture has had a positive impact on others in the class.

❖━━━━━━━━━━❖

**Explain concepts that are new to parents.** Give parents background information that you take for granted. For example, explain the concepts of cooperative learning, math manipulatives, and thinking skills activities, and discuss your school's reading program. Describe the reading instruction that the student is receiving and tell what subjects he or she leaves your classroom for. American school life holds many mysteries for newcomers' parents, and learning about them only through a child's reports can lead to misunderstandings.

**Encourage parents to maintain and develop the home language.** Encourage parents to involve themselves in their child's education. Suggest that parents read with their child in the home language, use the home language to teach life skills and concepts to their children, discuss events and news with them, and maintain contacts with relatives and events in their home country. Encourage parents to ask their child about the new things learned each day and to provide assistance with homework.

Ask parents if they have access to children's books in their home language. If they do not have a public library card, explain how to get one. (A library may be a novel concept to people from less developed areas.)

> It is *not* helpful to ask parents to speak English to their children at home. This can undermine the quality of parent-child conversations and interfere with the teaching of values that the parents do best in their home language. The goal is to have the child become bilingual, not to lose his or her home language.

**Ask parents to help increase their child's exposure to English.** You might also suggest that parents encourage their child to join a baseball league, a scouting troop, or the Y, where he or she will receive increased exposure to English. Mention one or two worthwhile television programs and the public channels, but caution parents to limit the amount of TV their child watches and to monitor the child's viewing. Explain that there are a lot of objectionable programs in this country.

**Find out more about your newcomers.** Ask parents questions to discover as much as you can about your students: *How does your son/daughter seem to like school? How long does he or she spend doing homework? How many brothers and sisters are there? How old are they? What time does your child go to sleep? What are his or her favorite activities after school? How much time is spent watching TV or playing video games? What difficulties does the student report?*

# USING BILINGUAL PARENT VOLUNTEERS

*Bilingual parent volunteers are a wonderful asset to any teacher that works with newcomers. Bilingual volunteers who speak the same languages as your newcomers are invaluable to you not only for their in-class assistance but for the services they provide outside of the classroom as well. If you are an ESL or bilingual teacher, you may already have a group of parent volunteers who help you in the classroom. If you are a mainstream teacher, you may have limited contact with bilingual parents. Here are some suggestions for starting a Parent Volunteer Program in your school.*

**Make the initial contact.** Contact an approachable parent to ask him or her to help you with your newcomers. Don't limit yourself to parents who have children in ESL. Bilingual parents whose children are not in an ESL program often show interest in volunteering to help newcomers. If you are a mainstream teacher, let the ESL teachers in your school know that you are interested in having a bilingual parent volunteer work in your room. They

will know what languages are spoken in the homes of students in other grades. It is quite possible that the ESL teacher will know the parents and feel comfortable asking them to volunteer. A cultural fair, a food festival, or a program where ESL students will be performing are good events at which to meet bilingual parents. Parent conferences offer another avenue through which to recruit volunteers. Don't turn anyone away because of low language proficiency. Let limited-English-proficient parents know that you welcome whatever help they can give.

**Ask for a commitment.** Ask volunteers to commit to a definite period of time. A semester usually works best for most volunteers; afterwards, they can renew their commitment if they wish. Let them know that regular participation is best for the students. If possible, recruit volunteers that can work with your newcomers for thirty minutes once a week (or more). Be sure they know to call the school if they can't come to a session.

**Consider training your parent volunteers.** If you are a mainstream teacher, you probably don't have time to organize, screen, and train a volunteer squad, but you may be able to recruit a colleague to do so. The ESL or bilingual teacher has the skills and knowledge to train volunteers to work with your newcomers.

**Be prepared for the volunteers.** Set up a schedule so that you know when a volunteer is coming. Be prepared for the volunteer; identify specific tasks you want him or her to do. Provide the volunteer with interesting and varied materials to use with the newcomers. The activity pages from this book are a good start. Give the volunteer concrete feedback during the first few sessions. If you want the volunteer to use positive rather than negative reinforcers, for example, let him or her know right away. If it is too distracting to have the volunteer work in your classroom, find a quiet place for the pair to work. Fourth-, fifth-, and sixth-grade teachers should ask that volunteers work outside the classroom; newcomers at this age are very self-conscious about receiving extra help. *Be sure the volunteer knows what to do in the event of a fire drill.*

Familiarize volunteers with the materials in the language learning area or box (see page T11), and train them in using the tape recorder and any other equipment which they may need. Volunteers should know that you will be busy teaching and won't be able to interrupt your class to discuss routine details with them. Make it clear, however, that they should inform you of any unusual circumstances that come to their attention. If your time is limited, communicate through written notes that you leave at the volunteers' work table. Be sure volunteers are aware of professional standards of confidentiality regarding the students they assist or any records they handle. Express to volunteers the value of their assistance to you, to the school, and to the students.

**Use parent volunteers outside the classroom as well.** Bilingual parent volunteers can also:

❖ help you determine your newcomers' oral and reading abilities in the first language.

❖ explain American school programs to new parents so that they better understand the general routine of the classroom.

❖ become a liaison between a new family and the school.

❖ help new arrivals with registration, inoculation, and health records.

❖ teach useful home-language phrases to teachers.

❖ interpret during parent-teacher conferences.

❖ translate school correspondence and other important messages.

❖ help with "sensitive" issues such as referral, retention, and social problems.

Working with bilingual parent volunteers can be a very rewarding experience for you, for your students, and for the parents who participate in the program.

# STRATEGIES FOR TWO-WAY COMMUNICATION

*Many people, particularly children, quickly acquire techniques for communicating across the language gap. Others need demonstrations and encouragement to use body language. You might want to share some of these suggestions with classroom buddies, cross-grade tutors, and volunteers, too.*

- ☑ Be an active listener. Give your full attention to the language learner and make every effort to understand his or her attempts to communicate.

- ☑ Be patient. Demonstrate your patience through your facial expression and body language.

- ☑ When speaking to newcomers, use objects, draw pictures, or mime actions to convey meaning.

- ☑ Encourage newcomers to act out or to draw pictures to get their meaning across.

- ☑ Acknowledge newcomers' attempts to communicate. Give feedback, nods of the head, encouragement, and praise.

- ☑ Speak at a slow-to-normal pace, in short sentences.

- ☑ Use simple sentence structure (subject/verb/object).

- ☑ Use high-frequency words; avoid idiomatic language.

- ☑ Use names of people rather than pronouns.

- ☑ Use full forms (*cannot, is not, did not,* etc.) rather than contractions. Contractions can cause great confusion for newcomers who are unable to distinguish subtle sounds. *Can't, isn't,* and *didn't* are easily misinterpreted as *can, is,* and *did.*

- ☑ Pause after phrases or short sentences, not after each word. You do not want to distort the rhythm of the language.

- ☑ Repeat cheerfully. Use the same simple words and sentence structures, actions, or demonstrations.

- ☑ Speak one-on-one to the newcomer rather than in front of the class at first. The anxiety of being in the spotlight often interferes with a newcomer's comprehension and ability to respond.

☑ Talk in a calm, quiet manner. A loud voice sounds angry and does not increase comprehension.

☑ Avoid using complex sentences and the passive voice.

☑ Check the listener's comprehension at frequent intervals. Asking "Do you understand?" is not a reliable check since students may nod that they understand when in actuality they don't. (In some cultures, it is rude to indicate that a person is not speaking clearly.)

☑ Teach the phrases "I don't understand," "Slowly, please," and "Please repeat."

☑ Write your communication on the chalkboard or on paper so that your students have visual as well as auditory input.

☑ Have students refer to a bilingual dictionary for abstract words that cannot be drawn or acted out. If students do not know how to use the dictionary, locate the word for them. (Most bilingual dictionaries have sample sentences for each of the different meanings of words.)

☑ Simplify messages whenever possible. Newcomers will not understand compound sentences that use multiple clauses and conjunctions. Break the message into smaller, manageable parts to give newcomers a better chance at comprehension.

☑ Don't insist that students make eye contact with you when you are speaking with them. Lowering the eyes when speaking to someone is a sign of respect in many cultures.

☑ Resist the urge to overcorrect errors in speaking. This will cause anxiety and reduce efforts to speak. Give indirect correction by repeating what the student said, using correct English.

☑ Join with the students in your class in learning a few words of the newcomer's home language. The second-language learners will appreciate your efforts and may even become more willing to risk speaking in English.

# ❖ INSTRUCTIONS FOR ❖ NEWCOMER ACTIVITY PAGES

The newcomer activities are flexible and are easily modified for students of different ability levels. Most of the activities can be made interactive by pairing newcomers with a buddy or cross-grade tutor. Newcomers need simple, repetitive activities to gain confidence in their ability to learn English. Provide aural input for them through audio tapes or peer tutors. Allow newcomers to listen and read along as many times as desired.

Students may do an activity more than once, and for different purposes, as their language level increases. Cross references to other related newcomer activity pages in this book are listed in the Contents (pages iii–viii). Also included in the Contents is a correlation of the newcomer activities to the PHR ESL Story Cards. These suggested uses of the newcomer activity pages and Story Cards will help you to teach, reinforce, and expand the language and content of your newcomer program.

It is not unusual for newcomers in the third to sixth grades to experience a silent period as they consciously or unconsciously delay speaking until they are comfortable. During this period, forcing speech production is counterproductive, as it raises anxiety levels and reduces the ability to focus on learning the meaning. The lower the anxiety level, the more language a student will absorb. Focus on helping students learn to recognize the names of the various vocabulary items and their meanings. When introducing new vocabulary to students, point to each item and say the word. If students are willing, have them repeat each word after you. If students are reluctant to speak, point to a few items, saying each word two or three times. Then ask students to point to each item as you name it. Be sure to acknowledge their efforts and accomplishments.

Most newcomers entering grades 3 through 6 have probably learned many of the basic concepts included in this book in their home language. You need only teach the language of the concept. However, keep in mind that schools in other countries have their own curriculums, and basic concepts and skills may be taught in an order different from that followed in the United States. Some newcomers, therefore, may not have what you consider to be grade-level skills and will need to learn both the concept and the language. You may also find newcomers who have had little or no formal schooling and have not developed literacy skills in their home language. Pages T24–T25 offer suggestions for working with preliterate newcomers.

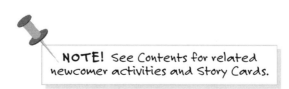

**NOTE!** See Contents for related newcomer activities and Story Cards.

## ❖ Screening for Newcomers ══════════════ Pages 1–2

TEACHER USES  To evaluate the newcomer's abilities in English  ❖  To provide a vehicle for establishing rapport with students

OBJECTIVES  To respond to oral questions and directions in nonverbal and verbal ways  ❖  To demonstrate knowledge of English

INSTRUCTIONS  Use with students whose English seems very limited. Through body language and facial expressions, try to convey that this is not a test. Allay students' anxiety by demonstrating, giving examples, and praising them for anything they might know.

Photocopy page 2 and color the boxes at the bottom before giving the page to students. As you ask each question on page 1, put a check in the correct column. Write any comments in the fourth column. Questions 2 through 5 will help you determine the student's aural comprehension of basic concepts and classroom directions. For questions 3 through 5, call out at random three to five numbers, five to ten letters, and three or four colors from page 2. If the student responds incorrectly to four consecutive items,

check "Does Not Understand" and move on to the next question. If the student successfully points to most of them, check "Completes Task." Questions 6 through 11 help you to evaluate a student's language production. Proceed to this section only if students were able to complete the tasks in questions 3 through 5. If a student cannot answer any questions, reassure him or her by saying, "That's OK, we will help you learn English." Smile and use body language to convey your readiness to help.

Students that complete all the tasks on this screening successfully should be evaluated by a certified ESL teacher with a standardized test for English.

After conducting the screening, you may want to file this page in the student's folder.

## ❖ Teacher's Observation Form ══════════════ Pages 3–5

TEACHER USES  To document student growth  ❖  To call attention to social or academic areas where teacher intervention or assistance may be needed  ❖  To assist in reporting on a student's progress at a parent conference

INSTRUCTIONS  Complete the Teacher's Observation Form after a new student has made an initial adjustment to your class (but within the first month) and at regular intervals thereafter. You might wish to use the form

before parent conferences to document the student's language development, academic growth, and social adjustment to your class. Keep in the student's folder.

## ❖ Home-Language Greeting ══════════════ Pages 6–7

TEACHER USES  To welcome newcomers to the school  ❖  To orient new students to the school  ❖  To allay student anxieties  ❖  To lay a foundation for building trust and rapport  ❖  To suggest good work habits

OBJECTIVE  To learn about the new school environment in the home language

INSTRUCTIONS FOR RECORDING THE GREETING  Read the greeting on pages 6 and 7. Modify it to reflect your school, making any appropriate additions or changes. Have bilingual volunteers translate the modified version of the greeting. Ask them to record the greeting in their home language and supply you with a written transcript. Make copies of the tapes to lend to new students, and keep the originals as master tapes. Carefully label all tapes.

Since the collecting of tapes in various languages can be costly and time-consuming, you might want to request the help of other teachers, or perhaps ask the PTA for a small grant. Share your tapes with colleagues and make copies of their master tapes for your audio library.

INSTRUCTIONS FOR USING THE GREETING  When newcomers arrive in your class, give them an opportunity to listen to the tape (using headphones) sometime during their first day. Allow them to listen to the tape again the second or third day as well, since there is a lot of information in the greeting. If no tape recording is available, send home a written translation for the parent to read with the child. In the absence of a translation, send home the English version.

## ❖ Student ID Card Page 8

TEACHER USE  To provide newcomers with an ID card during their first days at school

OBJECTIVES  To fill out an ID card ❖ To learn one's address, phone number, and other identifying information ❖ To respond to oral questions

INSTRUCTIONS  On the first day of class, help students prepare an ID card. Give students the opportunity to fill out the card on their own. Pair students who need help with a buddy. Ask the buddy to read the ID card to the newcomer and to fill it out with the newcomer's information. (You will need to provide buddies with this information.) Tell the newcomer to copy the information on the blank ID card at the bottom of the page. Ask the student to bring a photo from home, if possible, to attach to the card.

If students are not reluctant to speak, have the buddy ask questions, such as *Where do you live? What's your phone number?*

Laminate the cards or attach them to index cards. Tell students to keep their ID card with them at all times. Make sure that each student is picked up after school or knows the way home.

You may wish to reuse this page when the student is able to fill out the card on his or her own, or when he or she is able to respond to oral questions.

## ❖ Welcome to Our School Pages 9–23

TEACHER USES  To provide students with "formulas" and high-frequency expressions that will enable them to communicate basic needs at school ❖ To introduce students to basic classroom directions ❖ To encourage interaction with others ❖ To suggest positive behaviors and good work habits

OBJECTIVES  To learn how to communicate basic needs at school ❖ To learn some English for socializing and interacting with others ❖ To become familiar with basic directions and expressions used in the school environment ❖ To relate speech to print ❖ To follow classroom directions

INSTRUCTIONS FOR MAKING AND RECORDING THE *WELCOME* BOOK *(See the next page for additional instructions for completing page 23, Rules for Fire Drills.)* Make a *Welcome* book for each newcomer by photocopying and then stapling together pages 9 through 23. Record the *Welcome* book on tape. The entire script (pages 9–23) may be read by one person using different voices, or by two to six people, each playing the role of one or more characters. Record the script at a slow-to-normal pace, allowing a short pause after each sentence. Be sure to state each frame number before reading the dialogue. Use a bell or whistle to indicate that the student is to turn the page. You may wish to record the *Welcome* book at a natural conversational pace as well, without the numbers or pauses. Introduce this more challenging version only after students have had the opportunity to listen to the slower recording. Make copies of the tape for student use, and keep the master tape in a safe place. Label all copies.

Most of the text can be understood through the pictures and through continued exposure to the real language of the classroom. However, you may want to have bilingual volunteers translate the script. Keep the original translations in a file and photocopy for student use. If possible, have the bilingual volunteers record the script (or parts of it) in their home language.

INSTRUCTIONS FOR USING THE *WELCOME* BOOK

- Present a copy of the *Welcome* book to new students. Have them listen to the cassette (using headphones) while following the pictures. Show students how to operate the tape recorder, use the pause button, rewind, etc. Allow them to decide whether to listen to a page repeatedly or to run through the entire script from beginning to end.

- Allow students to listen to the slower-paced recording of the *Welcome* book once or twice daily, as long as needed.

- Give some of the classroom commands and instructions that appear in the *Welcome* book. Demonstrate what to do or how to respond if students seem uncertain. Have students reenact some of the dialogues. Praise students for their comprehension.

- Have students listen to the naturally-paced recording, following the pictures.

- Have students listen to the home-language recording of the *Welcome* book.

- Have students make a map of the school, labeling the bathrooms, the water fountains, the school office, the nurse's office, and various classrooms.

- In your daily instructions to the class, try to use the same phraseology found in the *Welcome* book. Note whether or not the new students are following the instructions with increased confidence.

## ❖ Rules for Fire Drills ━━━━━━━━━━━━━━━━━━━━━━━━━━ Page 23

OBJECTIVES  To learn about fire drills and safety procedures for leaving the building ❖ To acquire new vocabulary

INSTRUCTIONS  Many schools around the world do not conduct fire drills. Therefore, the loud noise of a fire alarm and the sudden rush to leave the building can be very frightening for newcomers. If possible, have students work on this page with a bilingual parent, cross-grade tutor, or buddy. Use frames 7 and 8 to write and illustrate additional rules or safety procedures followed in your school. Ask the bilingual volunteers to relay the information to the newcomers.

Once the page has been presented and reviewed in the students' home languages, read the captions as you point to the pictures. Have students indicate the correct picture as you read the captions a second time. Have students copy the sentences into their notebooks.

EXTENSION  Have students draw a picture of a fire drill at your school. Tell them to write about the fire drill and safety procedures in their first language. Ask a bilingual buddy or volunteer to make sure their written description conveys an understanding of fire drill procedures.

## ❖ New People in My Life ━━━━━━━━━━━━━━━━━━━━━━━━ Pages 24–28

TEACHER USES  To welcome newcomers to your classroom ❖ To foster positive relationships between newcomers and their classmates ❖ To involve the entire class in easing the newcomer's adjustment

OBJECTIVES  To become acquainted with classmates and learn their names ❖ To use visual cues to read sentences ❖ To relate speech to print

INSTRUCTIONS FOR MAKING AND RECORDING THE *NEW PEOPLE IN MY LIFE* BOOK  Involve the entire class in making the *New People in My Life* book. Photocopy pages 26 to 28 as many times as necessary. Cut each page into strips. For page 26, distribute one strip to each student in your class. Show the class the sample strips on page 25. Ask students to draw a self-portrait or tape a school photo in the space provided. Have students carefully print their names on the first line and

then write one sentence that tells of their interests, hobbies, talents, or pets on the second line. Ask them to illustrate their sentences. Fill out your strip for page 27. Have students in the class make strips for the gym, art, music, ESL, and other teachers. (Example: *This is Miss Clark. She is the music teacher.*) Ask volunteers to make strips for the principal, secretary, nurse, custodians, aides, cafeteria workers, and crossing guards to be included on page 28, "Other People." Have students glue the strips to the appropriate page and then order the pages. For the cover of the book (page 24), use copies of the photos or self-portraits from the individual strips. Make enough copies of the book for your newcomers. File the master copy for future use. Have new arrivals add their strips to the master copy.

Ask each student to tape record his or her part of the book. Make copies of the tape for student use, and keep the master copy in a safe place. Label all copies

INSTRUCTIONS FOR USING THE *NEW PEOPLE IN MY LIFE* BOOK
- Have newcomers listen to the tape and read along in the book as many times as desired

over several days or weeks.
- Newcomers can alphabetize classmates' names, categorize students by gender, add their own names and sentences to the book, color the pictures, and copy the sentences into a notebook.
- Have newcomers work with a buddy or in small groups to respond to students' questions. Supply a few model questions to get students started. (Examples: *Who has a dog? Who is from China?*) Allow newcomers to point to the appropriate student.
- Encourage newcomers to thank classmates for making the book.

## ❖ The Alphabet ═══════════════════════════════ Pages 29–31

OBJECTIVES  To learn the names of the letters in the Roman alphabet
  ❖ To practice writing upper- and lowercase letters

INSTRUCTIONS  (The alphabet activities in this book have been designed for preliterate newcomers and those students who are not familiar with the Roman alphabet.) Introduce each letter by saying the name and pointing to it. If possible, present new letters to students in the context of their name, a classmate's name, or other familiar word. Have students repeat the letters as you say them aloud. (Remember not to force students who are not ready for oral language production to repeat. Instead, ask

them to point to the letters that you name.) As you introduce a new letter, review previously-taught letters by asking students to point to the letter you say. Have students use these pages to practice the formation of each letter.

For additional practice with the formation of letters, have students work on ruled paper that is appropriate to their grade level. Teach students to recognize key words used in your handwriting program such as *uppercase* and *lowercase*.

## ❖ The Cursive Alphabet ═══════════════════════ Pages 32–33

OBJECTIVES  To practice writing upper- and lowercase letters in cursive  ❖ To relate cursive letters to printed letters  ❖ To demonstrate recognition of cursive letters

INSTRUCTIONS  (These exercises are particularly useful for preliterate students and those newcomers who are not familiar with the Roman alphabet.) Newcomers in grades three and up will be surrounded by cursive writing from their very first day. Since students will gain much self-confidence from being able to read and write in cursive like their classmates, you will want to introduce the cursive alphabet soon after they have mastered print. Pace your instruction so as not to overwhelm students; newcomers whose first language uses a non-Roman alphabet will need to learn all four sets of symbols.

Introduce the cursive alphabet by placing the strips of letters from page 32 next to their print counterparts. Ask students to point to the

letters you say. Students will require a lot of practice when learning to write in cursive. Make practice pages by attaching two strips of letters from page 32 to a copy of page 33. Photocopy the page for students. To allow for practice of all upper- and lowercase cursive letters, you will need to make four pages.

EXTENSIONS  Using the cursive letters on page 32 and the print letters on pages 29 to 31, make flash cards. Have newcomers play concentration games, matching print to cursive, cursive lowercase to cursive uppercase, or print lowercase to print uppercase.

Have students use cursive letters when making the Dictionary Cards (pages 34–35).

OBJECTIVES  To associate letters of the alphabet with words that begin with those letters  ❖  To recognize sound-symbol correspondence  ❖  To copy vocabulary words

INSTRUCTIONS  (This activity is particularly useful for preliterate students and those newcomers not familiar with the Roman alphabet.) Read aloud the letters of the alphabet and demonstrate their sounds using a picture dictionary or words from the vocabulary cards (pages 49–50, 56–57, 64, 69, 155–157, 161) in this book. Help students to complete page 34. Draw students' attention to the lower- and uppercase letters in the corner of each box. Help students find a word for each letter, using the vocabulary cards in this book or a picture dictionary. Ask newcomers to write the word they have selected in the space provided and then draw a picture of it. Make 4 photocopies of page 35 and have students fill in the remaining letters of the alphabet. For each letter, have them find a word, write the word, and then draw a picture.

Once students have made a set of dictionary cards, involve them in a variety of activities. In small groups, have newcomers cut out their cards and arrange them in alphabetical order. (You might want to use photocopies of the cards so that students can keep the original pages in their folders.) As students acquire new vocabulary words, have them create additional dictionary cards. Newcomers can also sort cards into different categories as their collection of cards grows.

EXTENSION  Photocopy page 35 for each letter of the alphabet. Have students find six words for each letter, write them on the lines, and then draw pictures to illustrate the words. Provide magazines or vocabulary cards from this book for students who prefer to cut out pictures. Staple the pages together to make an alphabet picture book.

OBJECTIVES  To count from one to forty in English  ❖  To demonstrate an understanding of number words

INSTRUCTIONS  Introduce the numbers from one to forty by naming each number in Part A. Ask students to point to each number that you call out. Have students practice counting from one to forty in English, and then by twos, threes, fives, and so forth. In Part B, tell students to

write the number for each number word.

For additional practice, have students make flash cards and concentration games using numbers and number words, or ask a classmate to dictate numbers to the newcomer.

OBJECTIVES  To acquire number vocabulary for counting up to one billion  ❖  To match numbers to number words

INSTRUCTIONS  (This page is designed to teach the English words for these numbers. Children who have not developed these number concepts in their home language will need additional help.) Introduce the numbers from one to one billion by naming each number in Part A. Ask students to point to each number that you call out. In Part B, have students draw lines to match the numbers to the number words.

For additional practice, have students make flash cards and concentration games using

numbers and number words. Enlist the aid of a classmate to dictate numbers to the newcomer.

For more activities with numbers, please see the math section of this book (pages 165–176).

EXTENSION  Make a page similar to Part B, using larger numbers. Keep numbers simple at first (*2,000; 300,000; 4,000; 11,000,000*).

NOTE! See Contents for related newcomer activities and Story Cards.

## ❖ Ordinal Numbers

OBJECTIVE  To acquire vocabulary for ordinal numbers

INSTRUCTIONS  Introduce students to the English words for ordinal numbers by naming the numbers in the box. Have students repeat after you. Then ask them to point to each number you say. Ask questions about the picture, such as *Who is first? third? second?* Have students answer by pointing to the correct answer or by naming the person. In Part B, help students read the questions and write the answers.

Extend the concept of ordinal numbers to other familiar groupings at school: subjects in the day, grades in school, row or group numbers, etc.

## ❖ Draw the Hands on the Clocks
Page 39

OBJECTIVE  To express time in English

INSTRUCTIONS  Review the number words for zero through sixty. Have students practice counting by fives. Work with a digital clock or watch, or a cardboard clock with movable hands. Move the hands on the clock and help students express the times in English.

Have students read the time statements below each clock and enter the correct time on the digital clock. Then ask students to draw the hands on the clocks. If appropriate, introduce additional time statements. (Examples: *It's twenty minutes after/past five. It's ten to three.*)

## ❖ What Time Is It?
Page 40

OBJECTIVE  To practice writing expressions of time in English

INSTRUCTIONS  For each example, have students first write the numerals in the digital clock and then write out the time expression on the appropriate line. You may wish to teach time expressions that include *quarter* and *half*.

## ❖ Calendar
Page 41

OBJECTIVES  To complete a calendar for the current month ❖ To name the days of the week ❖ To talk about dates in English ❖ To review ordinal numbers

INSTRUCTIONS  Use the calendar to introduce the names of the days of the week. Have students fill in the calendar for the current month. Then use the page to elicit vocabulary. Ask questions such as the following: *What is the date today? What day of the week is today? What day of the week was yesterday? What day of the week will tomorrow be? Point to the second Tuesday. Find the seventeenth day of the month; what day is it?* Ask classmates to make up questions that include the dates of holidays and special events.

EXTENSIONS  Have students use the calendar to record the weather during the course of a month. Use the weather icons from page 143.

Have students use the calendar to record special and/or routine events, such as classmates' birthdays, class field trips, soccer practice, and music lessons. Students might use icons, words, or a combination.

## ❖ What Day Is It?
Page 42

OBJECTIVES  To practice writing and spelling the days of the week ❖ To respond to questions about the days of the week

INSTRUCTIONS  In Part A, have students unscramble the names of the days of the week, referring to the words in the word box. Then help them read and respond to the questions in Part B. Introduce the concept of *weekend*.

Invite students to draw and label something they do on the weekend.

You may wish to ask newcomers questions 2, 3, and 4 each day to reinforce the vocabulary.

## ❖❖ Months of the Year Cards ══════════════════════ Page 43

OBJECTIVES  To name the months of the year ❖ To write the months in order

INSTRUCTIONS  It is very challenging to represent months of the year in a culture- and climate-free way. April is not rainy in all parts of the country, and not all schools begin in September. You may wish to have students in your class redesign some of the Months Cards so that they reflect the weather, activities, and holidays in your area of the country.

Help students learn to say the months of the year. Then have them write the names of the months in order, using the cards as a reference. Ask students to cut the cards apart and glue them on index cards. Suggest that they put them in order, use them as flash cards or for concentration games, or sort them by weather and seasons.

Ask students what holidays occur in their home countries in a particular month. Then have them tell you in what month a particular holiday (i.e., Thanksgiving, Cinco de mayo, Ramadan) falls.

## ❖❖ What Month Is It? ══════════════════════ Page 44

OBJECTIVES  To practice writing and spelling the months of the year
❖ To respond to questions about the months of the year

INSTRUCTIONS  Have students unscramble the names of the months in Part A. Show them how to use the word box to help. You may wish to do an example on the board. Help students read and respond to the questions in Part B.

## ❖❖ Birthday Survey ══════════════════════ Pages 45–46

OBJECTIVES  To review the months of the year ❖ To relate speech to print
❖ To conduct a survey ❖ To interpret the results of a survey ❖ To create a chart to display the results

INSTRUCTIONS  Photocopy the survey on page 45. Have students practice the question they will ask. (*When is your birthday?*) If necessary, have a bilingual buddy work with the newcomer. Encourage the students being surveyed to make sure that their response is recorded correctly.

When the survey is complete, ask newcomers to answer the questions on page 46. Teach the necessary vocabulary: *fewest, most, more*. Have students make a chart of the results of their survey. Display the chart in the classroom.

## ❖❖ Color Words-1 ══════════════════════ Page 47

TEACHER USE  To provide a reference page of color words for students
OBJECTIVES  To match colors to color words ❖ To label using color words
❖ To complete sentences using color words

INSTRUCTIONS  Provide students with the crayons needed to complete Part A. Encourage students to find the color word on each crayon and to match it to the corresponding word on the chart. Have students color the crayons accordingly. Ask them to name the colors as they work. Encourage students to add and label any missing colors. Have newcomers point to each color as a buddy calls out color words. In Part B, have students complete the sentences. Accept any reasonable response.

## ❖❖ Color Words-2 ══════════════════════ Page 48

OBJECTIVE  To match colors to color words
INSTRUCTIONS  Have students color the circles as directed, leaving the numbers visible.

Tell students to color the picture by number.

EXTENSION Use color words in the context of familiar vocabulary. Ask questions, such as *What color is your shirt? What color is the pencil?*

Accept one-word answers in the beginning, and encourage students to use short phrases or sentences as they acquire more language.

## ❖ Clothing Cards

TEACHER USE To provide reference pages for the clothing activities in this book

OBJECTIVES To acquire basic clothing vocabulary ❖ To write sentences using clothing words ❖ To respond to questions about clothing

INSTRUCTIONS Teach the vocabulary in groups of five to ten words, depending on the age and ability levels of your students. Say each word and pause, allowing students to repeat if they wish. Encourage them to write the home-language word (using a bilingual dictionary, if necessary) for each picture on the page. Pair students who are not literate or who don't know how to use a dictionary with a bilingual buddy. Ask students to point to each item on the page as you name it. Then ask students to name the items that you point to.

Provide students with a second set of cards to make flash cards or concentration games, or to use in the bingo game on page 51. You might also have students sort cards by weather or season.

Students who are ready to read and write can use the Clothing Cards as a basis for reading and writing activities. Have students write sentences using a frame that you provide: *This is a hat . These are socks .*

If students are ready, provide a model question-and-answer conversation starter on the chalkboard: *Are you wearing a dress today? Yes, I am./No, I am not.* Pair newcomers with classmates to practice asking and answering the questions. To encourage further interaction with students in the class, provide another communicative conversation starter: *What are you wearing today? I'm wearing a _____ .*

You may wish to provide students with a folder for keeping their clothing pages so that they are readily available during subsequent activities.

EXTENSIONS Students may wish to add their own clothing cards. Encourage them to draw and label any personally relevant vocabulary items, i.e., *earmuffs, barrettes, cardigan sweater, hooded jacket, ID bracelet.*

Introduce vocabulary such as *polka-dots, stripes, solid colors, plaid, checkered,* and *flowered.*

## ❖ Game Board

OBJECTIVE To demonstrate aural comprehension of vocabulary words

INSTRUCTIONS Make enough copies of the game board for each newcomer to have at least one board. Designate a total of forty of the vocabulary cards from this book that students can use to make their game board. (See the Clothing Cards [pages 49–50], Food Cards [pages 56–57], Verbs Cards [page 64], and Animal Cards [pages 155–157, 161]. When photocopying the page, you may wish to enlarge the game board to accommodate some of the larger vocabulary cards.) Have each student select 24 of the 40 cards, color the pictures, arrange the cards as they wish on the game board, and then glue them in place.

Place your forty cards into a box. Invite a buddy or cross-grade tutor to act as the first caller.

Instruct the caller to choose a card at random and call out the pictured item. Show students how to mark their board with a paper clip or small paper square if the item is on their game board. The first student to complete a vertical, horizontal, or diagonal row calls out "bingo." Have the student read back the names of the pictured items in the row. After a few games, invite the winner to become the next caller.

Another version of this game is to have students write a vocabulary word from the cards in each square on the board. Have the caller show the picture (covering the word) and name the pictured item. Have students mark the word if it appears on their board.

PRENTICE HALL REGENTS ESL NEWCOMER PROGRAM, GRADES 3 – 6
T51

## ❖ Pack for a Trip ══════════════════════════ Page 52

OBJECTIVES  To organize clothing according to weather conditions and recreational activities  ❖  To express choices through drawing or writing

INSTRUCTIONS  Invite students to select a place they would like to go. Show pictures from calendars, magazines, or brochures to spark interest and encourage imagination. Places might include the beach, an amusement park, the mountains, Disney World, a lake or river, a nearby city, or the student's home country. Have students write the name of the place on the line at the top of the page. (If students are unable to choose, pick a location that is popular in your area of the country.)

Tell students to consider the activities they will be involved in (i.e., camping, skiing, swimming) as well as seasonal and weather conditions. (Use the weather pictures on pages 137 and 138 to help students understand the kind of weather they may need to pack for.)

Have students use the Clothing Cards to decide what they will need to pack. Students who have difficulty writing should glue pictures from the Clothing Cards on the page. Others should write the names of items they have chosen to pack. If students wish to include toiletries or items of clothing not pictured on the cards, have them draw and then label a picture of each item.

On a separate sheet of paper, have students write short sentences about what they packed. Tell them to use color words. (Example: *I packed a red shirt in my suitcase.*) Encourage students to talk about what they have packed with a buddy or cross-grade tutor.

## ❖ What Will You Wear? ══════════════════════ Pages 53–54

OBJECTIVES  To select clothing based on weather and recreational activities  ❖  To label a picture

INSTRUCTIONS  Help students read and understand the sentences in each box. Use the weather pictures from pages 137 and 138 to increase comprehension. Have students draw and color a picture of themselves in each of the four contexts. Then tell students to label the clothing they are wearing, referring to the Clothing Cards if necessary. Have students add color words.

Recruit a buddy or a cross-grade tutor to ask questions about the drawings, such as *Are you going to school? Is your umbrella blue? Is it snowing? What color is your raincoat?*

EXTENSION  Have students write sentences about their pictures. Give them a frame: *When it's [sunny/hot/raining/snowing], I wear _____ . When I go [to school/to the beach/ outside], I wear _____ .*

## ❖ Clothing Survey ═══════════════════════════ Page 55

OBJECTIVES  To conduct an observation survey  ❖  To write sentences with clothing vocabulary  ❖  To respond to questions about classmates

INSTRUCTIONS  Review the vocabulary at the top of the page with students. Help them read and understand the sentences. You may wish to highlight the clothing word in each sentence for preliterate students and those who need more guidance. Show students how to do the first example. Tell them to look around the room for a classmate who is wearing earrings. Have them note the sample sentence. The page has been designed for students to complete independently. However, if you wish to render

the activity more interactive, have a buddy ask the newcomer questions, such as *Who is wearing earrings?* If newcomers are unsure of a student's name, have them point to the student in question. The buddy can supply the name.

NOTE! See Contents for related newcomer activities and Story Cards.

T52            PRENTICE HALL REGENTS ESL  NEWCOMER PROGRAM, GRADES 3 – 6

TEACHER USE  To provide reference pages for the food activities in this book

OBJECTIVES  To acquire basic food vocabulary  ❖  To write sentences using food words  ❖  To respond to questions about food

INSTRUCTIONS  Teach the vocabulary in groups of five to ten words, depending on the age and ability levels of your students. Have students write the home-language word (using a bilingual dictionary, if necessary) for each picture on the page. Pair students who are not literate or who don't know how to use a dictionary with a bilingual buddy. Say each word and pause, allowing students to repeat if they wish. Then ask students to point to each item on the page as you name it. Next, have students name items as you point to them.

After students color and cut out the cards, encourage them to draw and label other foods using the blank cards provided. Students may wish to draw foods from their home countries.

Provide students with a second set of cards to make flash cards or concentration games, or to use in the bingo game on page 51.

Students who are ready to read and write can use the Food Cards as a basis for reading and writing activities. Have students write sentences using a frame that you provide: *This is a  tomato . These are  eggs .*

If students seem ready, provide a model question-and-answer conversation starter on the chalkboard: *Do you like  bananas  ? Yes, I do./No, I don't.* Pair newcomers with classmates to practice asking and answering the questions. To encourage further interaction with students in the class, provide another communicative conversation starter: *What is your favorite vegetable?*

You may wish to provide students with a folder for keeping their food pages so that they are readily available during subsequent activities.

EXTENSIONS  On a large sheet of paper, outline a food pyramid. Have students sort the Food Cards into the correct food groups and then glue them on the pyramid. This is an excellent buddy or small group project. Knowledge of basic food vocabulary and concepts will enable newcomers to participate in regular classroom instruction on health and nutrition.

Have students develop illustrated menus. Ask them to sort food items into the three meals of the day. Teach *breakfast, lunch,* and *dinner* using time indicators.

## ❖❖ *My Feelings about Foods* ══════════════════════════════════ Page 58

OBJECTIVES  To sort illustrated food words into categories along a continuum according to preference  ❖  To develop vocabulary for expressing likes and dislikes  ❖  To copy food words

INSTRUCTIONS  Have students sort twelve to twenty Food Cards into the four categories on the page. Tell them to copy the name of each food in the correct column.

Provide four sentence frames for speaking and writing: *I like _____ . I don't like _____ . I hate _____ . I love _____ .*

## ❖❖ *Plan a Meal* ══════════════════════════════════════════════ Page 59

OBJECTIVES  To acquire vocabulary for the items in a place setting  ❖  To practice using food vocabulary  ❖  To plan a balanced meal  ❖  To label a picture

INSTRUCTIONS  Introduce vocabulary for items in a place setting. Name each item and pause, allowing students to repeat if they wish. Ask students to point to items as you name them. Help them label the picture using the word box. Next, have students draw a healthy

breakfast, lunch, or dinner on the page. Tell them to label the food, referring to the Food Cards on pages 56 and 57, if necessary.

EXTENSION  Have students draw their favorite meal or a holiday meal from their home country. Ask them to write a sentence about it.

## ◆ Favorite Fruit Survey ═══════════════════════════════ Pages 60–61

OBJECTIVES  To acquire fruit vocabulary ❖ To conduct a survey ❖ To organize
data in a graph ❖ To answer questions using a graph

INSTRUCTIONS  Help students practice asking the question at the top of page 60. Encourage students in the class to help newcomers record the responses by writing their initials or making a check in the correct box. Help newcomers transfer the results from the survey to the bar graph on page 61. When the bar graph is completed, have students answer the questions in Part B. Provide students with a frame for writing sentences: [Name of student]'s *favorite fruit is* _____ .

## ◆ Where Is It? ════════════════════════════════════════ Page 62

OBJECTIVE  To demonstrate an understanding of place prepositions

INSTRUCTIONS  Use small objects and manipulatives to introduce the place prepositions *in, on, under, next to, over, behind,* and *between.* Demonstrate first, then give students directions such as *Put the pencil in the box, Put the crayon on the box, Put the paper under the box, Put the scissors next to the box, Put your hand over the box.* Keep in mind that you are teaching the vocabulary for describing spatial relationships in English, not the concept of spatial relationships, which third to sixth graders will have already learned in their home language. It is important to remember that not all place prepositions are easily translated from language to language.

Have students color, cut out, and then glue the birds in the picture. They may color the pictures if they wish. Have them copy the six sentences into their notebooks.

## ◆ Where Will You Draw It? ════════════════════════════ Page 63

OBJECTIVES  To demonstrate an understanding of place prepositions
❖ To identify place prepositions in a sentence

INSTRUCTIONS  Review the vocabulary on the page. Have students follow the directions, drawing the items in the correct places. Have a buddy read the directions to preliterate newcomers and demonstrate what to do. The students may color the picture, and then write sentences about the picture. Ask them to underline the words that tell *where* in each of the sentences.

## ◆ Verb Cards ═════════════════════════════════════════ Page 64

TEACHER USE  To provide a reference page for the action word activities in this book

OBJECTIVES  To acquire basic action word vocabulary ❖ To write sentences using action words ❖ To respond to questions

INSTRUCTIONS  Teach the vocabulary in groups of five to ten words, depending on the age and ability levels of your students. Have students write the home-language word (using a bilingual dictionary, if necessary) for each picture on the page. Pair students who are not literate or who don't know how to use a dictionary with a bilingual buddy. Say each word and pause, allowing students to repeat if they wish. Ask students to point to each picture on the page as you name the action. Then have students call out the action word for each picture that you indicate.

Provide students with a second set of cards to make flash cards or concentration games, or to use in the bingo game on page 51. You might also have students group cards to show actions they perform at school and actions they do at home.

Students who are ready to read and write can use the Verbs Cards as a basis for reading and writing activities. Have students write sentences using a frame that you provide: *The boy/girl can  run .*

If students seem ready, provide a question-and-answer model on the chalkboard: *Is the girl  running ? Yes, she is./No, she isn't.* Pair newcomers with classmates to practice asking and answering the questions. To encourage further interaction with students in the class, provide a communicative conversation starter: *Do you like to  run ? Yes, I do./No, I don't.*

You may wish to provide students with a folder for keeping their verb pages so that they are readily available during subsequent activities.

EXTENSIONS Have students add other action words such as *laugh, cry, throw, catch, cut,* *close, push,* and *pull.* Use pictures from sports and entertainment magazines to illustrate additional words.

Have students use the verbs to describe what classmates are doing. (Examples: *Juan is singing. Karen is talking.*)

Ask students to sort the cards into different categories: time of day (in the morning, in the afternoon, at night); place (on the playground, at school, at home, in gym class). After students have grouped the cards, ask *when* and *where* questions, such as *When do you sleep? Where do you read?* Encourage students to respond using phrases. (Examples: *in the morning, at school*) To review expressions of time, elicit specific times to *when* questions. (Example: *at 8:00*)

❖◆ *Action Words* ═══════════════════════════════════ Page 65

OBJECTIVES To demonstrate an understanding of action verbs ❖ To express meaning through mime ❖ To complete written sentences ❖ To express meaning through drawings

INSTRUCTIONS Review the vocabulary words in Part A. If students need assistance as they work on the sentences in Part B, mime an action to elicit the answer. Have students copy the sentences on a separate sheet of paper and then draw pictures at the bottom of page 65 for two of the sentences.

EXTENSION Compile a list of twenty to thirty common action words that are relevant to your students (i.e., *wave, sing, sneeze, cough*). Teach students to respond to each word with a specific movement or action. For example, when you call out "Wave," have students respond by waving their hands in the air. When students are beginning to respond correctly to most of the words, play a game with them. Have students sit around a table. Call out a series of actions such as "Wave, jump, cry" and have students take turns responding without speaking. If the first student cannot complete the three actions in the order given, move around the circle to the next student. Do not repeat the command until everyone in the circle has had a chance to act out the words. This is a good activity for working on memory and aural comprehension.

❖◆ *Noun or Verb?* ═══════════════════════════════════ Page 66

OBJECTIVES To classify words as *nouns* or *verbs* ❖ To copy words

INSTRUCTIONS Review the vocabulary in the center of the page with students. Help students distinguish between nouns and verbs. Offer a few examples to be sure that students understand what to do. Have preliterate students place the Clothing and Verbs Cards (pages 49–50 and 64, respectively) on the table. Tell them to sort the cards and then copy (or dictate) each word in the correct column.

❖◆ *More Than One* ═══════════════════════════════════ Page 67

OBJECTIVE To use the plural forms of regular and irregular nouns

INSTRUCTIONS Elicit from students the vocabulary word for each picture shown in the word box. Repeat the singular and plural forms several times. Hold up fingers to show *one* and *more than one*. Some students will experience difficulty in aurally discriminating regular plurals from their singular counterparts (*hand/hands*), particularly if in their first language there is no plural form or the final "s" is not pronounced. Help students read the words at the bottom of the page and write the plural form of each noun.

Suggest that students who need additional practice with these plural nouns cut out the pictures and glue them on 2" x 3" pieces of construction paper or oak tag. Have students spread the cards out on the table and point to the picture that you name.

Have students make cards of both the plural and singular forms of the nouns and use them to make flash cards or a concentration game.

## ❖ My School ═══════════════════════════════ Page 68

OBJECTIVES  To learn information about the new school  ❖  To complete a form

INSTRUCTIONS  Before photocopying this page, you may wish to include additional information about your school (i.e., the school motto, school colors, mascots, sports teams). Help newcomers read and complete the sentences. Have them look up any unknown words in their bilingual dictionaries. (If applicable to your school, ask buddies to show students where the teachers' names are posted or written outside the classroom doors. Have newcomers take a quick trip to the art, music, and other classrooms to copy the teachers' names.) Refer students to the School Activity Cards on page 69 as they write the names of other classes.

## ❖ School Activity Cards ═══════════════════════ Page 69

OBJECTIVE  To acquire vocabulary for school subjects and activities

INSTRUCTIONS  Select only those activities that are relevant to your school and students. Point to each activity card and repeat the activity word several times. Demonstrate the meaning, using objects and realia from around the room. To demonstrate social studies, for example, you might hold up the social studies textbook or a map used in class. Have students draw and label three activities at the bottom of the page. Additions may include recess, health, assembly, drama, chorus, band, and so forth. If necessary, have a bilingual cross-grade tutor or parent volunteer write each word in the student's home language. These cards may be used to make bingo (page 51) or concentration games.

## ❖ Daily Schedule ═══════════════════════════ Page 70

OBJECTIVES  To make a daily schedule  ❖  To practice using vocabulary for school subjects and activities  ❖  To practice using expressions of time

INSTRUCTIONS  Make five copies of this schedule for each newcomer. Tell students that they will make a schedule for each day of the school week. Have them write a different day at the top of each schedule. Ask students to cut out the School Activity Cards from page 69 and to lay them out on their desk. Have students work with a buddy to find the appropriate activities for each day. Students can copy the names and/or the icons for each relevant activity on the schedule. Tell them to write the time of each activity on the clock to the left. Have students keep these schedules at the front of their notebooks.

EXTENSIONS  Have students write sentences about the schedule. Provide them with an example such as *On Mondays, I go to gym at 10:30.*

Send students home with a blank schedule to chart after-school or weekend activities. Refer students to the In the Park (pages 117–120) and Around the Town (pages 121–125) scenes as well as the family activities (pages 126–128) and Things to Do pages (pages 129–130).

**NOTE!** See Contents for related newcomer activities and Story Cards.

OBJECTIVES  To acquire vocabulary related to the surrounding school and community environments ❖ To demonstrate an understanding of spoken language ❖ To begin to develop reading skills ❖ To relate speech to print ❖ To complete passages using newly acquired vocabulary

GENERAL INSTRUCTIONS  There are twelve full-page pictures in this section; ten are school scenes and two are community scenes. Each scene is followed by activity pages that help teach and reinforce the vocabulary and sentence structures. Before assigning the activity pages to newcomers, use the full-page picture to teach the needed vocabulary. Point to items (the lunch bag, for example) or actions (standing in line, for example) in the scene, repeating the vocabulary words several times. Use realia and mime to increase comprehension. To evaluate the newcomers' understanding of vocabulary, ask them to point to items or actions as you name them. When students are beginning to assimilate vocabulary, ask them to name each item that you point to.

Help students learn to read the names of the students in the scenes. They appear repeatedly throughout the scenes and provide clues for understanding the text. The girls are Akiko, Carmen, Jennifer, Mei, Nadia, and Shantra. The boys are Alain, Joe, Miguel, Palo, Po Wen, and Tan.

EXTENSIONS  Ask students to draw a picture of the art classroom, the nurse's office, the library, etc. at your school. Have them label objects and people. Encourage students to share their drawings with a buddy or in a small group. Have them write sentences about their pictures. Post the student pictures around the classroom.

Invite students to draw a picture of the art classroom, the nurse's office, the library, etc. in the school they attended in their home country. Ask questions about the school, such as *Was there a lunchroom in your school? Was there a nurse?* Encourage newcomers to describe what is happening in their drawing.

ACTIVITY TYPES  Each of the twelve scenes is followed by several of the following activity types.

❖══════════❖

***Look, listen, and read***  Read, or have a buddy read, the text in this section. The text describes what is happening in the full-page scene. Have newcomers follow along as the text is read to them. Have them refer to the scene to identify the actions being described. Give students the opportunity to listen to the text a second and possibly third time. (You may want to record the scene texts on tapes.)

Ask students simple yes/no questions, such as *Is Miguel reading?* Progress to either/or questions, such as *Is Shantra reading or writing?* Finally, for those students who seem ready, ask *what, where, when,* and *why* questions, such as *What is Nadia doing? Why is Mei raising her hand?* Remember not to force oral language production. If a student is reluctant to speak, do not require that he or she respond verbally.

❖══════════❖

***Yes or No activities***  There are two types of Yes or No activities; students are asked to either check the correct column or circle the correct response. Be sure students understand the directions before beginning the activity. Help students read each sentence. Demonstrate how to find the answer in the *Look, listen, and read* text.

❖══════════❖

***Matching activities***  In the first type of matching activity, students are asked to match pictures to words. Show students where to write the correct letters.

The second type of matching activity requires students to complete sentences by matching a character to the action that he or she is performing. Sentences are picked up directly from the *Look, listen, and read* text. Show students how to scan the text to find the answers. When students have completed the activity, have them copy the sentences into their notebooks.

The last type of matching activity appears on page 124. Students are asked to match town places to activities common to those places. Make sure that students understand the vocabulary in the phrases before attempting the exercise. Use visual aids and mime to communicate meaning.

Often, there is more than one correct answer for an item in a matching activity. Accept any reasonable response. However, you may want to take this opportunity to teach strategies for considering all possibilities before making a final decision. On page 124, for example, there are two correct possibilities for a place to buy boots, the department store or the shoe store. If students select the former, ask them to find another place to buy boots.

**Listen, read, and write**  Have students locate and underline each word from the word box in the *Look, listen, and read* text. Then read the *Look, listen, and read* text slowly. Have students write the missing words on the lines. Suggest that they refer to the word box for help. Allow students to refer back to the complete text, if necessary.

When students are familiar with the text, have them complete the cloze activity again, as you read the paragraph at a faster, more natural speed.

Have students copy the paragraph to practice letter formation, spelling, word spacing, punctuation, and fine motor skills. Ask a classmate to check the newcomer's paragraph for accuracy.

**Coloring activities**  Review clothing and color vocabulary. Have students color the scenes according to the directions. Help them read the sentences, if necessary.

**Draw a picture activities**  Help students read the word or sentence in each frame. Have them draw a picture to illustrate it. On page 76, encourage students to draw and label other classroom objects in the three empty frames.

**Word searches**  Many students will not have experience with this type of word puzzle. Demonstrate how to search the puzzle vertically, horizontally, and diagonally to find the words listed at the top of the page. Encourage students to cross out words at the top of the page as they find them in the puzzle. In some of the puzzles, there are a few words that have not been introduced in the text for that scene. The Library word search, for example, contains *fact, fiction, card,* and *borrow.* You may wish to teach such high-frequency words in addition to the scene vocabulary. Students may enjoy pointing out other familiar words that they find. (See page T71 for answer keys.)

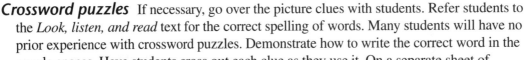

**Crossword puzzles**  If necessary, go over the picture clues with students. Refer students to the *Look, listen, and read* text for the correct spelling of words. Many students will have no prior experience with crossword puzzles. Demonstrate how to write the correct word in the puzzle spaces. Have students cross out each clue as they use it. On a separate sheet of paper, have students write an original sentence, or one from the text, for each item.

**Answers for the crossword puzzle on page 106**  ACROSS  3. note  5. thermometer  6. scale  7. knee  8. mouth  9. Band-Aid  DOWN  1. elbow  2. ice pack  3. nurse  4. headache  5. telephone

**Answers for the crossword puzzle on page 111**  ACROSS  6. cage  8. terrarium  9. turtle  10. penguin  12. feeding  13. whale  15. rabbit  DOWN  1. dolphin  2. writing  3. iguana  4. reading  5. computer  7. drawing  8. teacher  11. animals  14. mice

***Sentence completion activities*** *(pages 77 and 115)* Review the labeled picture at the top of the page, naming each object several times. Ask students to point to each item that you call out.

For page 77, you may wish to have newcomers take a tour of the bathroom (with an adult). Reinforce vocabulary from the page, and foster good hygiene practices by including a demonstration of *flush* and *wash*. If appropriate, show female students where to get sanitary products or how to use the vending machine. Make sure students know how to ask to go to the bathroom.

For page 115, have newcomers visit the computer room. Review the vocabulary by having students match the pictures on page 115 with the actual objects.

***Label and list activity*** *(page 125)* Ask students to look at each picture. Have them write the name of the store below the picture. Invite students to look at a picture dictionary and to refer to their Clothing and Food Cards (pages 49–50 and 56–57, respectively) to list items that can be bought at each store.

## ◆ Family Picture ═══════════════════════════════════════════ Page 126

OBJECTIVES  To acquire family vocabulary  ◆  To share information about one's family  ◆  To label a picture

INSTRUCTIONS  Introduce basic family vocabulary (i.e., *mother, father, brother, sister*) using a picture of your family or a picture of a student's family. If neither is available, use the picture of the family on page 127. Then have students draw a picture of their family. Most students will draw only the immediate family. Encourage them to include their extended family by asking *Does your mother have a mother? Does your father have a brother?* If possible, find out about your student's family situation ahead of time so that you can be sensitive to family make-up. Some families have been separated by divorce or death. Some students may have a single parent, stepbrothers and stepsisters, or a grandparent as the primary caretaker. Refer to the student's records to find out as much as you can.

## ◆ Family Fun ═══════════════════════════════════════════════ Page 127

OBJECTIVE  To explore family relationships in English

INSTRUCTIONS  Use the picture at the top of the page to review family relationships. Then have students cut out the individual pictures and glue each one on a separate square of construction paper. Each student will need his or her own set of cards. Using a set of cards, reconstruct the family tree on a table or desk. Ask students questions, such as *Who is Juan's mother? Who is Juan's sister?* Introduce new vocabulary (i.e., *cousin, niece, uncle*) using the familiar family words: *Who is Juan's mother's brother?* When students respond, ask the question again, this time substituting the word *uncle. Who is Juan's uncle?* Keep in mind that words such as *cousin, brother, aunt,* and *uncle* may not necessarily have the same meaning when translated to English.

EXTENSION  Play a game with students. Sitting around a table, have students hold all their family cards. Tell students not to show their cards to other players. Create riddles about various family members. Begin with clues such as *Show me Juan's mother (Rosa)* and progress to clues such as *Who is the mother's mother? (Inez)* and *Who is the mother's mother's husband? (Rodrigo)* Students find the cards and place them face down in front of them on the table. On the count of three, everyone turns their cards face up, allowing you to quickly see who has understood the lesson. Students do not have to speak to demonstrate their understanding of the lesson. As students progress in oral language development, allow them to give clues to their classmates.

## ❖ Who Are These People?

Page 128

OBJECTIVES  To identify family members  ❖  To complete written sentences

INSTRUCTIONS  Use the picture at the top of the page to review family relationships and vocabulary. Photocopy page 127 for students and demonstrate how to refer to the family tree to complete the sentences on page 128. You may wish to have newcomers work with a buddy or in a small group.

## ❖ Things to Do

Pages 129–130

OBJECTIVES  To acquire vocabulary for recreational activities  ❖  To express preferences  ❖  To label a picture  ❖  To express oneself through drawing

INSTRUCTIONS  Use realia and mime to help students understand each of the activities depicted on page 129. Have students point to or tell which of the activities they like to do and which ones they don't like to do. Ask students to cut out the pictures and sort them several ways: Activities I like to do alone/Activities I like to do with others; Activities I do with friends/Activities I do with my family. You may wish to copy the continuum on page 58 and have students chart their preferences.

On page 130, have students draw and label other activities that they enjoy. If students cannot label the pictures themselves, have them dictate to a buddy. Before or after the activity, expand student's vocabulary, introducing additional recreational activities such as *going to the mall, going to the movies, playing video games,* and *talking on the telephone.*

## ❖ Safety Signs

Pages 131–132

OBJECTIVES  To learn about safety rules and precautions  ❖  To associate common safety signs with their meanings  ❖  To illustrate captions

INSTRUCTIONS  Signs presented here will probably be new to students. Use mime and realia to help students understand the signs on page 131. If possible, have a bilingual buddy, cross-grade tutor, or parent work with newcomers to explain important information in the home language. You may want to take newcomers on a mini field trip in and around the school to look for these signs. When they return from the trip, have students tell where they found each sign.

Familiarize students with other signs: Do Not Enter, One Way, Fire Exit, Out of Order, Do Not Run, Slippery When Wet, Stop, Wheelchair Access, and No Trespassing. Ask students to draw three additional signs at the bottom of page 131. These do not have to be safety signs.

On page 132, help students match each sentence with a sign. Make sure students understand all of the signs. Talk with students about safety issues such as using a helmet when riding a bike or skating, not talking to strangers, dialing 911 in emergencies, and not taking drugs. Have students draw two safety signs at the bottom of the page. They may want to label the signs in their home language.

## ❖ The Flag of the United States

Page 133

OBJECTIVES  To learn about the American flag  ❖  To answer questions about the flag  ❖  To compare the American flag with the flag of one's home country

INSTRUCTIONS  Introduce the vocabulary words *stars, stripes,* and *states.* Have students color the flag as indicated and then complete the sentences. Be sure students understand that the word *American* refers to the United States. Encourage practice with oral language production by asking students questions such as *How many states are there? What color is the American flag?*

Have students draw and color the flag of their home country. Ask newcomers to share their drawing with a buddy or a small group of students. Encourage newcomers to write a few sentences about the flag. Display the flag drawings.

## ❖ The Pledge of Allegiance

**OBJECTIVES** To learn the Pledge of Allegiance ❖ To participate in classroom activities

**INSTRUCTIONS** Most students will want to recite the Pledge of Allegiance, eager to be involved in classroom activities. (Remember that some newcomers have religious or cultural backgrounds that preclude their participation in this activity. Do not require that they recite along with the other students. Teach them to be respectful of their classmates and to stand quietly during the Pledge.) If possible, have a bilingual parent, cross-grade tutor, or buddy explain the Pledge of Allegiance to newcomers. Read the text on page 134 and have students follow along. You, or a volunteer, may wish to record the Pledge of Allegiance on tape. Allow students to listen to the tape as many times as necessary.

Have students color the picture, copy the text, look up words in their bilingual dictionaries, and make flash cards of unfamiliar words.

## ❖ The United States of America

**OBJECTIVES** To acquire basic vocabulary and knowledge about the United States ❖ To use map-reading skills ❖ To complete sentences

**INSTRUCTIONS** Help students locate their home countries, North America, and the United States on a globe. Demonstrate the meaning of *continent* by tracing North America and the continents of your students' home countries with your finger. Demonstrate the meaning of *country* by tracing around students' home countries and the United States. Point out the three ways of referring to the United States: *the USA, the United States,* and *the United States of America.* Using the globe, indicate the three bodies of water that touch the United States. Then, call out countries and bodies of water and have students point to them on page 135. Help students locate the equator and north/south poles on the globe. Introduce vocabulary used to express direction: *north, south, east,* and *west.*

Have students look at the vocabulary in the word box on page 136. Ask them to locate and underline each word from the box in the text on page 135. Next, have students use their bilingual dictionaries to look up the words. Encourage them to note the definitions. Help students read and complete the sentences in Part B. Tell them to use page 135 to check their answers.

**EXTENSION** Using an atlas, have students draw a map of their home country. Have them label the continent, country names, and major bodies of water. Suggest that students label the capital of the country as well. Have students write short sentences about their home county using the text on page 135 as a model. (Example: *This is the continent of Asia. South Korea is a country in Asia.*) Have newcomers share their drawings and descriptions with a buddy or a small group of students. Display their work in the classroom.

## ❖ What's the Weather?

**OBJECTIVES** To acquire weather vocabulary and expressions ❖ To relate speech to print

**INSTRUCTIONS** Point to each picture and say the appropriate weather expression. Have newcomers repeat after you. (Remember not to force students to repeat if they are not ready for oral language production.) Then ask students to point to each picture that you describe. You may wish to record these two pages on tape. Allow students to listen to the tape as many times as they wish.

The weather pictures can be cut apart and glued on 3" x 5" index cards to be used as flash cards. Have students copy the weather expression on the back of the card and glue the picture (with no text) on the front. If appropriate, provide additional weather vocabulary on the board for students (i.e., *rain, wind, snow, sleet, hail, clouds, sun*).

Pair students with a buddy to practice using weather expressions. You may want to introduce the question *What's the weather today?* to engage students in a conversation.

# ❖ What's the Temperature?

**OBJECTIVES** To read a thermometer using the Fahrenheit scale ❖ To express the temperature in Fahrenheit

**INSTRUCTIONS** Provide a small thermometer for hands-on observation and hang a larger thermometer outside your classroom window. Newcomers are likely to be familiar with the Celsius scale but will need practice reading the Fahrenheit scale. Provide the language needed to express temperature readings in words. Have students notice that the "F" represents Fahrenheit and that the ( ˚ ) represents degrees.

Place a thermometer in a cold glass of water. Have students observe the lowering of the alcohol. Ask students to note what happens when the thermometer is removed from the water and then held in their hands or under their arms. Point out that the thermometer measures up to 120 degrees.

Have students complete frames 1 through 4, drawing figures in the latter two to illustrate the concepts of *warm* and *cool.* Help students understand the four vocabulary words—*cold, hot, warm,* and *cool*—in terms of the weather in your part of the country. Help them also understand that the four words change in meaning across seasons; the *warm* of the winter is not the same *warm* of the summer. In other words, *warm* may simply imply an increase in temperature and *cool* a decrease in temperature. Have students refer to outdoor and indoor thermometers to answer the questions and record the temperatures in frames 5 and 6. Encourage students to illustrate their answers.

# ❖ Today's Weather

**OBJECTIVES** To demonstrate comprehension of weather vocabulary ❖ To record the weather ❖ To write a weather report

**INSTRUCTIONS** Have students record their weather observations by checking off the appropriate boxes and filling in the thermometer. Have students note the time of day of the temperature reading. In Part B, ask students to use the information from Part A to write a weather report. Have students share their reports with a buddy.

**EXTENSION** Videotape a television weather report in the morning and have students watch the tape. Replay the report, asking students to note the weather and temperature forecasts. Using their weather report from Part B, have students compare the television forecast with the actual weather and temperature.

# ❖ Yesterday's Weather

**OBJECTIVES** To demonstrate comprehension of weather vocabulary ❖ To record yesterday's weather ❖ To write a weather report ❖ To talk about the weather using the past tense ❖ To read a newspaper weather report

**INSTRUCTIONS** Have students record their weather observations by checking off the appropriate boxes and filling in the thermometer. Have students note the time of day of the temperature reading. In Part B, ask students to use the information from Part A to write a weather report. Have students share their reports with a buddy. Check to see that newcomers are reporting the weather using the past tense.

You might wish to have students complete this activity using a weather report from the newspaper. First show students how to find the weather report in the newspaper. Next, have students note the weather features and check off the appropriate boxes on this page. Then have them copy the temperature to complete the thermometer.

**NOTE!** See Contents for related newcomer activities and Story Cards.

OBJECTIVES  To predict the weather  ❖  To write a weather forecast
❖ To compare predictions with the actual weather

INSTRUCTIONS  Have students record their weather predictions by checking off the appropriate boxes and filling in the thermometer. In Part B, ask students to use the information from Part A to write a weather forecast. Have students share their forecasts with a buddy. Check to see that newcomers are predicting the weather using the future tense.

Have students check the weather the following day and compare it to their forecasts. To reinforce vocabulary, engage students in a two-week project of forecasting and then checking the weather.

OBJECTIVES  To observe the weather over a three-week period  ❖  To record temperature readings on a graph  ❖  To make a weather calendar  ❖  To answer questions and complete sentences using weather and temperature charts

INSTRUCTIONS  Have students read Part A on page 143 and notice the sample temperature graph. Help students begin their own temperature graphs by writing the dates for the next three weeks across the bottom of the chart on page 144. Each day at the same time, have students read the outdoor thermometer and record the temperature reading on their chart. Ask students to note the temperatures over the weekends and record them on Monday mornings. Have students draw lines to connect the temperature readings. When the graph is completed, have students observe the temperature changes. Ask: *Was there a general trend of warming or cooling? What was the hottest temperature? What was the coldest temperature?* If you wish to have students record the temperature for a longer period, tape several copies of the chart together.

Review the weather vocabulary in Part B on page 143. Familiarize students with the icons. Have students observe and record the weather for a three-week period using page 145. (Each newcomer will need three copies of this page.) For each day, have students write the date, record the temperature, and keep track of the weather using the icons shown on page 143. Encourage students to write something about the weather in the space provided. Ask questions, such as *Did it snow yesterday? Is it raining today? Will it snow tomorrow?* At the end of the three-week period, help students make a bar graph using the data they collected. Have them count the total number of days for each weather condition and record it on a separate sheet of paper. For example, if there were three snowy days, have students draw three snow icons next to the word *Snowy*. (Another alternative is to have students glue copies of the icons shown on page 143 next to the appropriate weather words.)

Using the temperature graph (page 144), weather calendar (page 145), and student-generated bar graph, have students answer the questions in Part C on page 143. Encourage students to add their own observations about the weather at the bottom of the page.

EXTENSION  Have students look at a weather map of the nation. Introduce any weather icons that are new to students. Ask questions, such as *What's the temperature in Boston? What's the weather like in Miami? Is it raining in Chicago?* If possible, find a listing of the temperatures in the home countries of newcomers. Have them answer questions about the weather there.

**NOTE!** See Contents for related newcomer activities and Story Cards.

## ❖ The Body

OBJECTIVES  To identify parts of the body ❖ To label a drawing of the body ❖ To associate parts of the body with action words

INSTRUCTIONS  Introduce the vocabulary by having students point to their own body as you name and indicate various body parts. Then have students identify the body parts on page 146 that you call out. Read the words at the top of the page with students. Have them label as many body parts as they can on their own. Then ask buddies to help newcomers finish the page.

Review the verbs on page 64. Teach new action words such as *smell, see, hop, bend, shrug, wave, hold,* and *wiggle,* demonstrating the meaning of each word. Ask students to alphabetically list the parts of the body in their notebooks. For each body part, have them write an action word. (Examples: *foot/run; knee/bend*)

EXTENSION  Have students divide a sheet of paper into three vertical columns with the headings "One," "Two," and "Ten." Have students write each body part in the appropriate column, using the correct singular or plural form. For example, below the "One" heading, students would write *neck,* below the "Two" heading, *arms,* and below the "Ten" heading, *toes.*

## ❖ The Face

Page 147

OBJECTIVES  To identify parts of the face ❖ To label a drawing of the face ❖ To associate parts of the face with action words

INSTRUCTIONS  Introduce the vocabulary by having students point to the parts of their face as you name and indicate them. Then ask students to point to each part of the face on page 147 as you name it. Read the words in the word boxes with students. Have them label as many parts of the face as they can on their own. Then ask buddies to help newcomers finish the page.

Teach new action words such as *see, smell, hear, taste, wink, chew, smile, kiss,* and *lick,* demonstrating the meaning of each word. Ask students to alphabetically list the parts of the face in their notebooks. For each part of the face, have them write an action word. (Examples: *lips/kiss; tongue/taste*)

EXTENSION  Have students divide a sheet of paper into two vertical columns with the headings "One" and "Two." Have students write each part of the face in the appropriate column, using the correct singular or plural form. For example, in the "One" column, students would write *nose,* and in the "Two" column, *eyes.*

## ❖ Look in the Mirror

Page 148

OBJECTIVES  To label a drawing of one's face ❖ To write a description noting physical characteristics

INSTRUCTIONS  Have each student draw and color a detailed picture of his or her face. Ask students to label the parts of the face using the vocabulary on page 147. Help them write a description at the bottom of the page.

EXTENSION  Provide students with another photocopy of this page, and have them draw and color a picture of a friend's face. Ask them to label the picture. Help students write sentences comparing the two pictures. Suggest that they use the model in Part B. (Example: *My eyes are green. Charles' eyes are blue. My hair is black. Charles' hair is blond.*)

NOTE! See Contents for related newcomer activities and Story Cards.

T64          PRENTICE HALL REGENTS ESL  NEWCOMER PROGRAM, GRADES 3 – 6

OBJECTIVES  To conduct an observation survey  ❖  To write sentences noting physical characteristics

INSTRUCTIONS  This is an observation survey. Begin by introducing (or reviewing) the vocabulary at the top of the page. Have students read each numbered item, look around the room to find a classmate who fits the description, and write a sentence in the space provided. Students may do this activity silently and independently. If you wish to render the activity more interactive, have newcomers ask questions such as *Who has brown eyes?* Encourage students in the class to respond to the questions.

EXTENSIONS  Expand students' vocabulary by providing additional descriptive words and phrases such as *blond hair, red hair,* and *freckles.*

Have newcomers compile information about classmates' physical characteristics. Start them off by writing a few questions on the chalkboard: *How many students have brown hair? black hair? straight hair? blue eyes?* Have students make a bar graph showing the results. Ask them to share the results in a small group of students. Encourage them to write sentences about the graph. (Examples: *Ten students have brown hair. Six students have blue eyes.*)

OBJECTIVE  To express common ailments

INSTRUCTIONS  Read, or have a buddy read, the sentences below each picture to newcomers. Have students repeat each sentence several times after you. Then read each sentence and have students point to the correct picture. Finally, read each sentence and have students mime the pain represented.

Engage students in pair work to practice using the vocabulary. Have one student read each sentence and the other mime the actions.

When they have worked with all eight expressions, have students switch roles.

EXTENSION  With students, compile a list of common ailments—*sore throat, toothache, stomachache, splinter, cut, bruise,* and so forth. Use mime and realia to demonstrate meaning. Introduce the following question-and-answer model for students to follow in practice conversations: *What's the matter? I have a  bruise .*

OBJECTIVES  To express conditions of health  ❖  To identify things to do for sickness and bodily injuries

INSTRUCTIONS  Introduce the expressions in Part A, using mime and exaggerated intonation. You may wish to have newcomers ask a few classmates *How do you feel?* If appropriate, teach additional expressions such as *I feel great/awful/ better/worse/OK/etc.*

For Part B, have students brainstorm other things to do when they are hurt or do not feel well—wash a cut, bandage the cut, go home and rest, visit the doctor, and so forth.

If newcomers do not understand vocabulary on this page, have them look up words in a bilin-

gual dictionary or have a bilingual parent or buddy translate. Have the newcomer note the vocabulary in his or her notebook, along with home-language translations and a drawing depicting each expression. Suggest that students keep this list handy to refer to when they are ill.

In Part C, encourage students to express their answers through words, drawings, or mime. Supply them with the vocabulary they need.

NOTE! See Contents for related newcomer activities and Story Cards.

Senses ═══════════════════════════════════════════════ Pages 152–154

OBJECTIVES  To acquire vocabulary associated with the five senses ❖ To respond
to questions through drawing ❖ To label a drawing

INSTRUCTIONS  Review the names of the pictured body parts and the meanings of the verbs *see, hear, smell, taste,* and *touch.* For each of the five senses, have newcomers draw and label things that can be sensed. Allow students to use their bilingual dictionaries, if necessary. Ask them to write a sentence for each picture. (Examples: *I can smell flowers. I can hear the birds.*)

For page 154, introduce the vocabulary at the top of the page using objects from around the classroom. Allow students to feel the objects as you describe them. Have students find other objects for each descriptive word and then draw pictures of six of the objects. Ask them to write a sentence for each picture.

❖ Animal Cards/Animal Body Parts Cards ═══════════════════ Pages 155–157

TEACHER USE  To provide reference pages for the animal activities in this book

OBJECTIVES  To acquire animal vocabulary ❖ To name animal body parts
❖ To write sentences about animals ❖ To respond to questions about animals

INSTRUCTIONS  Teach the vocabulary in groups of five to ten words, depending on the age and ability levels of your students. Have students write the home-language word (using a bilingual dictionary, if necessary) for each animal or body part on the page. Pair students who are not literate or who don't know how to use a dictionary with a bilingual buddy. Have students repeat each vocabulary word after you. (Remember not to force students who are not ready for oral language production to repeat.) Ask students to point to each animal (or body part) as you name it. Then have students name the items that you indicate.

Provide students with a second set of cards to cut apart and color. Supply a picture dictionary or encyclopedia for newcomers to use to research the colors of animals that they are unfamiliar with. Have students use this set to make flash cards or concentration games, or to use in the bingo game on page 51.

Students who are ready to read and write can use the Animal Cards and Animal Body Parts Cards as a basis for reading and writing activities. Have students write sentences using frames that you provide: *Whales live in the ocean . / Seals have flippers .*

Pair students with a buddy, cross-grade tutor, or volunteer to have them practice using the animal vocabulary. Tell the buddy to begin with yes/no questions, such as *Does a lion eat plants? Does a deer have feathers?* Beginning students may respond with "No." If appropriate, have the volunteer continue with either/or questions, such as *Does a deer have fur or feathers? Does a lion eat plants or animals or both?*

You may wish to provide students with a folder for keeping their animal pages so that they are readily available during subsequent animal activities.

EXTENSION  For the animal body parts page, have students add other words to describe animals, such as *skin, hair, webbed feet, claws,* and *whiskers.*

❖ Tell About These Animals ═══════════════════════════════ Page 158

OBJECTIVES  To identify animal body parts ❖ To label a drawing of an animal
❖ To describe a picture

INSTRUCTIONS  Review the animal body parts on this page. Have students label the three drawings. Ask them to talk about their pictures

with a buddy. Provide them with a model sentence for describing the animals: *A turtle has a shell , a tail , and claws .*

## ❖ How Do Animals Move? Page 159

OBJECTIVES  To categorize animals by the way they move  ❖  To copy animal words

INSTRUCTIONS  Act out the meaning of each column heading. Have students first sort the Animals Cards (pages 155–156) into the four groups. Next, have them copy the animal names in the correct columns. Point out that some animals move in more than one way. Ask students to note which animals belong in two (or more) columns.

EXTENSION  Teach a few additional verbs related to animal movement such as *crawl* and *slither*. Have students identify the animal(s) that each verb describes.

## ❖ What Animals Go Together? Page 160

OBJECTIVES  To classify animals into scientific categories  ❖  To copy animal words  ❖  To write sentences

INSTRUCTIONS  Teach the meaning of each heading using the Animal Cards (pages 155–156) or other pictures of animals. To introduce *mammal,* for example, show three or four pictures of typical mammals, drawing students' attention to the fur. Allow students to use bilingual dictionaries. Suggest that they write a home-language translation below each heading. Have students sort their Animal Cards into the six groups.  Then have them copy the names of the animals in the correct columns. Ask students into which category humans fall.

Provide a frame for students to write about the different animals: *A  lion  is a  mammal* .

## ❖ Animal Homes and Habitats Cards Page 161

TEACHER USE  To provide reference pages for the animal activities in this book

OBJECTIVES  To name animal habitats  ❖  To associate animals with their habitats  ❖  To write sentences about animals and their habitats

INSTRUCTIONS  As you point to each picture, name the habitat. Say each word and pause, allowing students to repeat if they wish. Tell newcomers to look up the words in a bilingual dictionary, or ask a bilingual cross-grade tutor or parent volunteer to translate them. Have newcomers point to each habitat as you call it out. Then indicate an item and elicit the vocabulary word from students. Ask what animals live there. Have students draw and label pictures of other habitats at the bottom of the page. Ideas include *the Arctic, tundra, jungle, pond, stream, lake, ocean, den, under a rock,* and *hive.*

Have students write a sentence for each picture using a frame that you provide:  *Birds  live in  nests* .

Provide students with a second set of cards to cut apart and color. Have them use this set to make flash cards or concentration games, or to use in the bingo game on page 51.

Have students keep this page in their folders for future reference.

## ❖ What Animals Live Here? Page 162

OBJECTIVES  To sort animals by habitat  ❖  To copy animal names

INSTRUCTIONS  Make several copies of this page. Have students place two habitat pictures from page 161 at the top of the page. Ask them to label the columns. (You might wish to tell students which cards to use: farm/zoo; desert/grass; tree/underground; etc.) Have students use the Animal Cards (pages 155–156) to find animals that live in each habitat. Ask them to copy the animal names in the correct column. Point out that some animals may fit into several groups. Offer as an example the lizard, which might be listed under forest, desert, or jungle.

## ❖ *What Do Animals Eat?* Page 163

OBJECTIVES  To sort animals into herbivores, carnivores, and omnivores
  ❖ To copy animal names  ❖ To write sentences about animals

INSTRUCTIONS  Explain the meaning of each heading by providing students with examples. Offer the deer as an example of herbivore, the lion as an example of carnivore, and the bear as an example of omnivore. Show students where to find this information if they do not know it. Allow them to work in pairs or small groups. Provide additional clues to distinguishing between the three types of animals.

For example, you might mention that it is likely that animals with large and pointed teeth are carnivores. Have students sort their Animal Cards into three groups and write each animal name in the correct column. If appropriate, have students write sentences about some of the animals. (Example: *The bear is an omnivore. It eats berries and fish.*)

## ❖ *What Animal Is This?* Page 164

OBJECTIVES  To research an animal  ❖ To write a short report on the animal

INSTRUCTIONS  Have students select an animal. Ask them to draw a picture of the animal in its habitat with its food. After students have named the animal, have them complete the sentences in Part B. Provide them with plenty of easy resource books for researching their animal. Encourage students

to work in pairs or small groups and to use bilingual dictionaries. This page can be used many times for different animals.

EXTENSION  Have students draw a picture of an animal from their home country. Ask them to describe the animal, its habitat, and food sources. Invite students to share their drawings.

## ❖ *Different Ways to Read Numbers* Page 165

OBJECTIVE  To read numbers in addresses, dates, telephone numbers, and prices

INSTRUCTIONS  Point out to students that numbers are often read in different ways. The numbers on doors, in telephone numbers, and in addresses, for example, are not read the same way as they are in math problems. Help students practice reading the numbers as written below the pictured items. Have students read the numbers at the bottom of the page to a buddy or cross-grade tutor.

EXTENSIONS  Bring in cash register receipts for students to read aloud.

Have students exchange ID cards (page 8) and read each other's addresses and telephone numbers aloud.

Have students make an address book with important emergency numbers. Then pair newcomers with buddies to practice reading the numbers aloud.

## ❖ *United States Coins* Page 166

OBJECTIVES  To identify and name U.S. coins  ❖ To demonstrate an understanding of the monetary value of each coin

INSTRUCTIONS  U.S. coins are confusing to newcomers. The values are not numerically indicated on the coins, and the smallest coin in the monetary system (dime) is twice the value of a larger coin (nickel). Use actual coins, if available, to teach the names and values of the *penny, nickel, dime, quarter, half-dollar,* and *silver dollar.* Help students learn to recognize

the coins from the heads and tail sides, as well as by the differences in size. Have students copy the names of the coins and write their values.

Ask questions, such as *How many nickels are in a quarter? How many dimes are in a half-dollar?* You may wish to have students use coins to show their answers.

## ❖ United States Bills ════════════════════════════════════ Page 167

OBJECTIVES  To identify and name U.S. bills  ❖  To demonstrate an understanding
of the monetary value of each bill

INSTRUCTIONS  Because they are all the same size and color, U.S. bills can be confusing to newcomers. Use the bills on this page to teach the names and values of the *one-dollar bill, five-dollar bill, ten-dollar bill, twenty-dollar bill,* and *one hundred-dollar bill.* Point out to students that the value is indicated numerically on the bills. Have students copy the names of the bills and write their values.

Ask questions, such as *How many five-dollar bills do you need to have twenty dollars? How many ten-dollar bills do you need to have one hundred dollars?* You might wish to use play money (or the bills from this page) to have students show answers to your questions.

## ❖ How Much Is It? ════════════════════════════════════ Page 168

OBJECTIVE  To determine the value of a group of coins

INSTRUCTIONS  On a table or desk, arrange a group of coins such as three nickels, two dimes, and a penny. Have students determine the total value. Repeat with other combinations of coins. Then have students complete this page.

## ❖ Going Shopping ════════════════════════════════════ Pages 169–170

OBJECTIVES  To write monetary values  ❖  To compare prices  ❖  To practice calculating monetary amounts  ❖  To acquire toy vocabulary

INSTRUCTIONS  Introduce the toy vocabulary on page 169. Say each toy word and pause, allowing students to repeat if they wish. Name each item and ask students to point to it. Indicate an item on the page and elicit the vocabulary word from students. Encourage students to color the picture.

When students are able to identify the pictured toys, ask them to read the amounts on the price tags. Next, demonstrate how to write the price on the line next to the appropriate word. If students are unsure of toy vocabulary, point out that the letters in the picture correspond to the letters in the activity.

Familiarize students with the vocabulary and types of questions they will find on page 170. Ask students to point to the item that is the most expensive and then the least expensive. Have students compare toys to determine which is more or less expensive. Ask either/or questions such as *Which is more expensive, the doll house or the drum?* Help students read and complete Part A.

Before attempting Parts B and C, pair newcomers with buddies to practice purchasing various toys and making change. Model bills can be made by mounting the illustrations from page 167. If possible, provide students with real coins.

## ❖ Shapes ════════════════════════════════════ Page 171

OBJECTIVES  To name common geometric shapes  ❖  To identify shapes in the environment

INSTRUCTIONS  Say the name of each shape several times as you point to it. Have students point to the shapes that you call out. (Students in the fifth and sixth grade will recognize most of these shapes and know the shape names in their home language. However, you may have to teach the concepts as well as the language to some third- and fourth-grade students.)

Then have students find an example of each shape in your classroom. Ask questions such as the following: *Does an octagon have eight sides? How many sides does a pentagon have? What shape has three sides?* Teach the terms *angle, perimeter,* and *circumference.*

Send newcomers on a scavenger hunt with a buddy around the classroom to complete Part A.

Tell students to draw and label an object that has each shape. Have them count sides and angles for each object. In Part B, have students draw a picture on the back of the page using all of the shapes. Encourage students to use their imagination. Have them label the shapes.

 ## Solid Shapes ======================================= Page 172

OBJECTIVES  To name and identify common solid geometric shapes
❖ To associate objects with solid shapes

INSTRUCTIONS  Say the name of each shape several times as you point to it. Have students point to the shapes that you call out. (Students in the fifth and sixth grade will recognize most of these shapes and know the shape names in their home language. However, you may have to teach the concepts as well as the language to some third- and fourth-grade students.)

Teach students how to count the surfaces of the solid shapes. Ask questions such as *How many surfaces does a cube have?*

In Part A, have students match each item with the shape name. In Part B, have students draw a picture on the back of the page using all of the shapes. Encourage students to use their imagination. Tell students to label the shapes.

## Lines ================================================= Page 173

OBJECTIVES  To identify and name mathematical lines

INSTRUCTIONS  Say the name of each type of line or ray as you point to its picture. Have students repeat if they wish. Ask students to point to each item in the word box as you name it. Indicate an item and elicit the

vocabulary word from students.

Have students draw lines in the spaces provided. To make the exercise more challenging, cover the examples at the top of the page.

## Measure in Inches ===================================== Page 174

OBJECTIVES  To measure using inches ❖ To write measurements using fractions

INSTRUCTIONS  Have students work with a buddy to find various lengths (i.e., one inch, six inches, nine inches) on a ruler. Have them measure a variety of classroom objects that are between one and twelve inches long. Draw students' attention to the half-inch, quarter-inch, eighth-inch, three-quarter-inch, five-eighths-inch, and seven-eighths-inch marks.

Have students complete the page. Invite students to write sentences about objects that they measured. Refer them to the model sentences in Part C.

Answers for Part B:  (1) 2 inches   (2) 1 3/4 inches   (3) 1 1/2 inches   (4) 2 1/4 inches (5) 2 1/2 inches.

## Measure Heights ====================================== Page 175

OBJECTIVES  To measure using feet ❖ To read a height chart ❖ To respond to questions about height

INSTRUCTIONS  Ask *How tall is Joe?* Draw students' attention to the measuring stick at the right and demonstrate how to use it to answer the question. Ask about each person in the picture. Have students complete the written activity.

EXTENSIONS  Provide a wall chart or tape measure and have students measure several classmates.

Use this opportunity to introduce some comparative and superlative words (*taller, shorter, tallest, shortest*). Ask questions, such as *Who is taller, Carmen or Mr. Nichols? Who is the shortest person in the picture?*

NOTE! See Contents for related newcomer activities and Story Cards.

OBJECTIVES  To demonstrate an understanding of linear measurement
❖ To measure oneself using feet and inches

INSTRUCTIONS  Have students use a tape measure to measure their height and the body parts listed. Allow them to work in pairs. Demonstrate *arm span* and *step* if students seem unclear. In questions 11 and 12, make sure students understand that they are comparing two things.

EXTENSION  Keep the page in the student's folder. At the end of the school year, have newcomers take the measurements again and compare the results with the first set of measurements, to see how they are growing and changing.

## Word Search Answer Keys

### Page 81

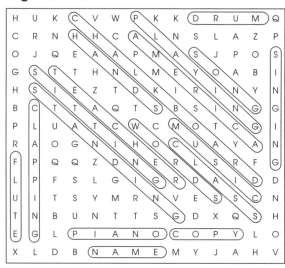

### Page 101

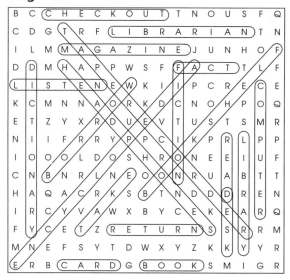

### Page 116

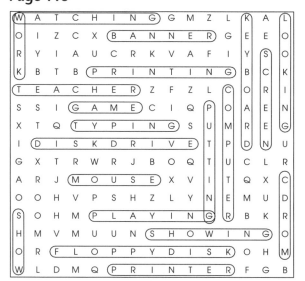

**NOTE!** See Contents for related newcomer activities and Story Cards.

Student's Name _____ Date _____

Interviewer _____

**Basic Comprehension** — Before you begin items 3 through 9, color the boxes at the bottom of page 2 red, blue, green, orange, brown, and yellow. Then use page 2 and the following questions and instructions with the newcomer.

| | Does Not Understand | Attempts Task | Completes Task | Interviewer Comments |
|---|---|---|---|---|
| **1.** What is your name? | | | | |
| **2.** Follow these directions. | | | | |
| Stand up. Sit down. | | | | |
| Clap your hands. | | | | |
| Touch your nose. | | | | |
| Point to your eyes. | | | | |
| **3.** Point to the number I say. | | | | |
| **4.** Point to the letter I say. | | | | |
| **5.** Point to the color I say. | | | | |
| **6.** Say each number I point to. | | | | |
| **7.** Say each letter I point to. | | | | |
| **8.** Say each color I point to. | | | | |
| **9.** Write your name. | | | | |
| **10.** How old are you? | | | | |
| **11.** What country are you from? | | | | |

Instructions: page T44

# Screening for Newcomers-2

## Number recognition

| | | | | | | |
|---|---|---|---|---|---|---|
| 2 | 7 | 9 | 0 | 14 | 6 | 10 |
| 13 | 20 | 36 | 43 | 25 | 32 | 58 |
| 45 | 71 | 57 | 64 | 82 | 79 | 63 |
| 86 | 102 | 98 | 116 | 200 | 95 | 150 |

## Letter recognition

| | | | | | | |
|---|---|---|---|---|---|---|
| a | B | c | D | e | F | g |
| H | i | J | k | L | m | N |
| o | P | q | R | s | T | u |
| V | w | X | y | Z | b | E |

## Color recognition

| | | | | | |
|---|---|---|---|---|---|
| | | | | | |

**Name** _____

Newcomer Program, Grades 3–6 • Prentice Hall Regents  © by Judie Haynes and Elizabeth Claire

# Teacher's Observation Form–1

Student's Name _____ Date _____

1. Home Language _____ Date of Birth _____

   Age _____ Sex ____

2. Date entered U.S. _____ Date entered this school _____

   Previous schooling in U.S.?   ☐ No
                                   ☐ Yes _____
   _____

3. Did the student study English in   ☐ No
   the home country?   ☐ Yes _____
   _____

4. Can the student read in the first   ☐ No
   language?   ☐ Yes _____

5. Is the student in an ESL class?   ☐ No
                                   ☐ Yes _____

6. Based on your experience with this student, rate the following.
   (0 = no English; 5 = native English)

   | | | | | | | | |
   |---|---|---|---|---|---|---|---|
   | a. seems to understand conversational English | 0 | 1 | 2 | 3 | 4 | 5 |
   | b. seems to understand content area lessons | 0 | 1 | 2 | 3 | 4 | 5 |
   | c. can decode grade-level texts orally | 0 | 1 | 2 | 3 | 4 | 5 |
   | d. can read grade-level texts with understanding | 0 | 1 | 2 | 3 | 4 | 5 |
   | e. has English writing skills | | | | | | |
   |     penmanship | 0 | 1 | 2 | 3 | 4 | 5 |
   |     spelling | 0 | 1 | 2 | 3 | 4 | 5 |
   |     sentence structure | 0 | 1 | 2 | 3 | 4 | 5 |
   |     speed | 0 | 1 | 2 | 3 | 4 | 5 |
   |     clarity of expression | 0 | 1 | 2 | 3 | 4 | 5 |
   | f. has English speaking skills | | | | | | |
   |     pronunciation and intonation | 0 | 1 | 2 | 3 | 4 | 5 |
   |     fluency | 0 | 1 | 2 | 3 | 4 | 5 |
   |     accuracy | 0 | 1 | 2 | 3 | 4 | 5 |

Instructions: page T44

## Teacher's Observation Form–2

7. How does this student's location in the classroom enhance his or her opportunities for observation and social interaction, and for peer or teacher assistance?

_____

_____

_____

8. What techniques for communication does the student utilize? (Check all that apply.)

_____ relies on interpreter

_____ gets assistance from teacher

_____ asks the other to repeat

_____ uses facial expressions, pointing, gesturing, acting

_____ draws pictures

_____ writes thoughts on paper

_____ uses dictionary

_____ repeats

_____ speaks carefully and clearly

9. With whom does this student seek to interact?

_____

_____

_____

10. What art, music, math, physical, social, and other strengths does the student have?

_____

_____

_____

11. What difficulties or weaknesses, other than language, does the student have?

_____

_____

_____

Newcomer Program, Grades 3–6 • Prentice Hall Regents    © by Judie Haynes and Elizabeth Claire

12. What are the student's interests and hobbies, reading preferences, goals, and motivators?

_____

_____

13. In what ways does the student's behavior seem to affect opportunities for socialization and growth in English?

_____

_____

14. Which of these responses do you see from classmates towards this student?

| _____ including | _____ willingness to help | _____ sympathy |
|---|---|---|
| _____ sharing | _____ protecting | _____ admiration |
| _____ imitating | _____ indifference | _____ annoyance |
| _____ hostility | _____ ridicule | _____ scapegoating |
| _____ envy | _____ resentment | _____ overprotective |
| _____ exploiting | _____ domineering | _____ excluding |

Comments _____

_____

_____

15. In what ways do the attitudes and behaviors of classmates toward this student seem to affect the opportunity for his or her growth in English?

_____

_____

16. What behavioral and other changes have you observed in the student as his or her language ability has further developed?

_____

_____

17. Other observations and comments

_____

_____

Newcomer Program, Grades 3–6 • Prentice Hall Regents © by Judie Haynes and Elizabeth Claire

Instructions: page T44

# Home-Language Greeting-1

## Tape Script

Hello. Welcome to _____ (*our school*).

We are happy to have you with us. Your teacher understands that you do not speak English. Everyone will try to help you. We made this tape to help you learn a little about your new school.

The name of the school is _____.

School begins at _____ every morning. Please come a little early.
School is over at _____.

Lunch is at _____. You can bring your lunch to school, or you can buy your lunch.

Lunch costs _____. Some students may receive a free lunch. The teacher will send home an application to your parents if you cannot pay for lunch. The teacher collects lunch money on _____.

(*Add details for milk money, etc.*) _____
_____
_____

If you need to go to the bathroom during class, ask the teacher for permission to leave the room. Say "Bathroom, please." or, "May I go to the bathroom?"

You will have a special class for _____ minutes every day (or, _____ _____) to help you learn English. This class is called ESL, or English as a Second Language. There are other students in the school who cannot speak English. The ESL teacher will come to your room and show you where that class will be.

You will have a language test to find out how much English you know now. Don't worry if you cannot answer any questions. Many other students have the same problem. At the end of the year, in June, the teacher will give you another test to see how much English you have learned. You will receive help in English as long as you need it.

(*Add, if appropriate.*) You will have a bilingual class every day to help you learn social studies, science, and math.

Newcomer Program, Grades 3–6 • Prentice Hall Regents  © by Judie Haynes and Elizabeth Claire

## Tape Script (*continued*)

There is gym class _____ a week. You will need _____
_____
_____
in gym class. Your teacher will tell you what day you have gym.

It's important to come to school ready to work. Go to bed early so you will have enough sleep each night. We hope you will eat a good breakfast in the morning before you come to school, too.

You need some basic materials for your school classes: _____
_____
_____

Ask your parents/guardians to let your teacher know if you cannot buy these things. Some may be available for you through the school.

Try to listen to the teacher as much as you can. Sometimes it will be impossible for you to understand the lessons. You can do other work then. You can look at pictures in your books. You can copy words from your dictionary. You can read a book in your language. You can keep a diary in your language of the new things you learn. You can write letters to your family and friends in your country. You can do work that the teacher gives you. A classmate may help you.

At first, you may get very tired of listening to English. It's OK to put your head down on your desk and rest for a while.

Many students like you have learned English in this school. It is a big job. You cannot do it all at once. But you can do it, little by little, day by day. It will be wonderful to know two languages, and we don't want you to forget your own language. Keep speaking your language with your family and friends.

We like our school. There are many good teachers and good programs. We all work together to keep the school clean and to make it a friendly place to learn.

The students in your class/school have prepared a *Welcome* book. They made a tape to help you learn many things in English. Look at the pictures as you listen to the tape. You can listen to it many times. You can rewind this tape and listen to it again, too. Good luck. We're glad you're with us!

Newcomer Program, Grades 3–6 • Prentice Hall Regents © by Judie Haynes and Elizabeth Claire

Instructions: page T44

## Student ID Card

School: _____ Grade: _____

Teacher: _____

Name: _____
                    (First)                         (Last)

Address: _____
                    (Street)                   (Apartment)

_____
(City)                            (State)     (Zip)

Telephone: ( _ _ _ ) _ _ _ _ – _ _ _ _ _

Date of birth: _ _ / _ _ / _ _    Sex: ☐ Male
                                        ☐ Female

Place of birth: _____

Nationality: _____ Language spoken: _____

Signature: _____ Date: _____

---

## Student ID Card

School: _____ Grade: _____

Teacher: _____

Name: _____
                    (First)                         (Last)

Address: _____
                    (Street)                   (Apartment)

_____
(City)                            (State)     (Zip)

Telephone: ( _ _ _ ) _ _ _ _ – _ _ _ _ _

Date of birth: _ _ / _ _ / _ _    Sex: ☐ Male
                                        ☐ Female

Place of birth: _____

Nationality: _____ Language spoken: _____

Signature: _____ Date: _____

Instructions: page T45

Newcomer Program, Grades 3–6 • Prentice Hall Regents    © by Judie Haynes and Elizabeth Claire

Instructions: page T45

Newcomer Program, Grades 3–6 • Prentice Hall Regents   © by Judie Haynes and Elizabeth Claire

Instructions: page T45

14

Newcomer Program, Grades 3–6 • Prentice Hall Regents   © by Judie Haynes and Elizabeth Claire

Instructions: page T45

16

Newcomer Program, Grades 3–6 • Prentice Hall Regents    © by Judie Haynes and Elizabeth Claire

Instructions: page T45

**44**

Can you help me, please?

Yes, what is it?

**45**

Let's use your dictionary.

I don't understand this.

**46**

Circle the answer.

3 + 4 =
a. 5
b. 6
c. 7
d. 8

**47**

Underline the answer.

3 + 4 =
5
6
7
8

**48**

Write the answer on the line.

3 + 4 = __7__

**49**

Fill in the blanks.

1. My name is __Carmen__.

2. I am __10__ years old.

3. I come from __Mexico__.

Newcomer Program, Grades 3–6 • Prentice Hall Regents   © by Judie Haynes and Elizabeth Claire

| 50 | 51 |
|---|---|
| Print your name. | Write your name in script. |
| <u>Akiko</u> | <u>Akiko</u> |

| 52 | 53 |
|---|---|

**52**

Copy the words five times each.

> boy
> girl
> English

**53**

Answer the question.

What's this?

<u>It's a chair.</u>

**54**

Draw a picture of a face.

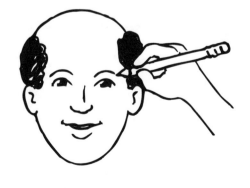

**55**

Label the parts of the face.

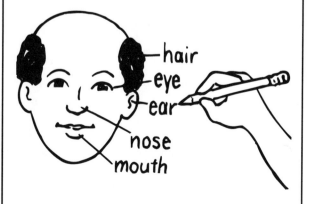

*Newcomer Program, Grades 3–6 • Prentice Hall Regents*

Instructions: page T45

Newcomer Program, Grades 3–6 • Prentice Hall Regents     © by Judie Haynes and Elizabeth Claire

Instructions: page T45

22

# Rules for Fire Drills

1

Fire

2

A Fire Drill

3

Listen to the teacher.

4

Leave your books.

5

Do not talk.

6

Walk quickly out of the school.
Do not run.

7

8

Instructions: page T46

# NEW PEOPLE
# IN MY LIFE

24

Newcomer Program, Grades 3–6 • Prentice Hall Regents    © by Judie Haynes and Elizabeth Claire

# My Classmates

My name is Joe.
I like baseball.

I'm Akiko.
My hobby is collecting coins.

Hi! My name is Shantra.
I have two dogs.

Welcome. I'm Mai.
I'm from China.

$7 \times 93 =$
8,462,738
4,925,217
3,826,990

$675\overline{)4392.67}$

My name is Tan.
My best subject is math.

Instructions: page T46

# My Classmates

Newcomer Program, Grades 3–6 • Prentice Hall Regents   © by Judie Haynes and Elizabeth Claire

# My Teachers

Newcomer Program, Grades 3–6 • Prentice Hall Regents  © by Judie Haynes and Elizabeth Claire

Instructions: page T46

# Other People

Newcomer Program, Grades 3–6 • Prentice Hall Regents    © by Judie Haynes and Elizabeth Claire

# The Alphabet – 1

Newcomer Program, Grades 3-6 • Prentice Hall Regents    © by Judie Haynes and Elizabeth Claire

Instructions: page T47

# The Alphabet – 2

J

j

K

k

L

l

M

m

N

n

O

o

P

p

Q

q

R

r

Newcomer Program, Grades 3-6 • Prentice Hall Regents    © by Judie Haynes and Elizabeth Claire

# The Alphabet – 3

S _____  s _____

T _____  t _____

U _____  u _____

V _____  v _____

W _____  w _____

X _____  x _____

Y _____  y _____

Z _____  z _____

Instructions: page T47

# The Cursive Alphabet – 1

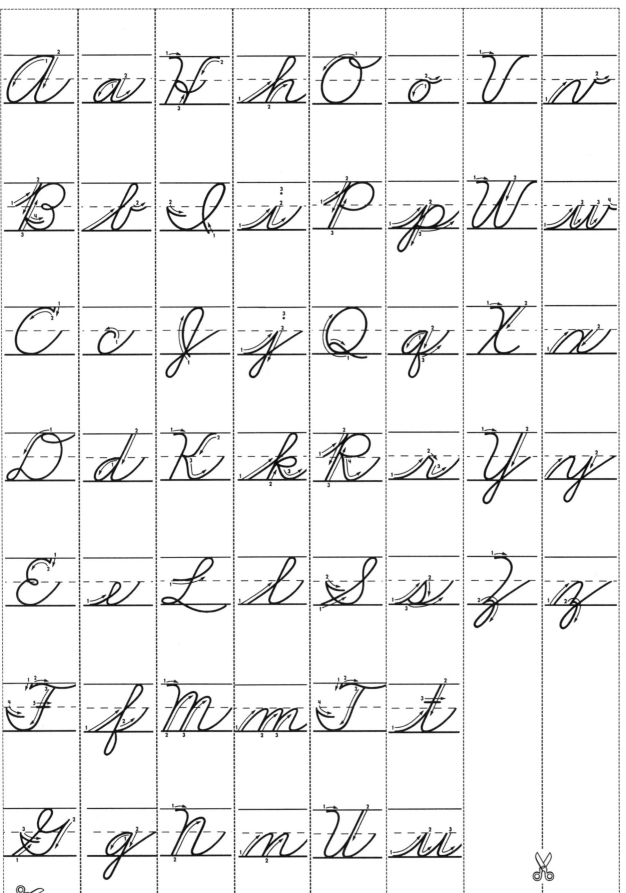

Newcomer Program, Grades 3-6 • Prentice Hall Regents    © by Judie Haynes and Elizabeth Claire

# The Cursive Alphabet – 2

Instructions: page T47

# Dictionary Cards – 1

**Write a word for each letter. Then draw a picture.**

A a

apple

B b

C c

D d

E e

F f

Newcomer Program, Grades 3-6 • Prentice Hall Regents   © by Judie Haynes and Elizabeth Claire

# Dictionary Cards – 2

**Write a word for each letter. Then draw a picture.**

Instructions: page T48

# Numbers – 1

## A. Listen, read, and count.

| | | | | | |
|---|---|---|---|---|---|
| 0 | zero | 8 | eight | 16 | sixteen |
| 1 | one | 9 | nine | 17 | seventeen |
| 2 | two | 10 | ten | 18 | eighteen |
| 3 | three | 11 | eleven | 19 | nineteen |
| 4 | four | 12 | twelve | 20 | twenty |
| 5 | five | 13 | thirteen | 21 | twenty-one |
| 6 | six | 14 | fourteen | 30 | thirty |
| 7 | seven | 15 | fifteen | 40 | forty |

## B. Write the numbers.

| | | |
|---|---|---|
| _____ two | _____ three | _____ four |
| _____ four | _____ six | _____ eight |
| _____ six | _____ nine | _____ twelve |
| _____ eight | _____ twelve | _____ sixteen |
| _____ ten | _____ fifteen | _____ twenty |
| _____ twelve | _____ eighteen | _____ twenty-four |
| _____ fourteen | _____ twenty-one | _____ twenty-eight |
| _____ sixteen | _____ twenty-four | _____ thirty-two |
| _____ eighteen | _____ twenty-seven | _____ thirty-six |
| _____ twenty | _____ thirty | _____ forty |

Newcomer Program, Grades 3-6 • Prentice Hall Regents    © by Judie Haynes and Elizabeth Claire

# Numbers – 2

## A. Listen, read, and count.

| | | | | | |
|---|---|---|---|---|---|
| 10 | ten | 60 | sixty | 1,000 | one thousand |
| 20 | twenty | 70 | seventy | 10,000 | ten thousand |
| 30 | thirty | 80 | eighty | 100,000 | one hundred thousand |
| 40 | forty | 90 | ninety | 1,000,000 | one million |
| 50 | fifty | 100 | one hundred | 1,000,000,000 | one billion |

## B. Match the numbers and words.

| | | | |
|---|---|---|---|
| nine | 18 | one hundred | 750 |
| eighteen | 36 | two hundred fifty | 1,000 |
| twenty-seven | 9 | five hundred | 250 |
| thirty-six | 45 | seven hundred fifty | 500 |
| forty-five | 27 | one thousand | 100 |
| fifty-four | 72 | ten thousand | 100,000 |
| sixty-three | 90 | fifty thousand | 10,000 |
| seventy-two | 63 | one hundred thousand | 1,000,000,000 |
| eighty-one | 54 | one million | 1,000,000 |
| ninety | 81 | one billion | 50,000 |

Newcomer Program, Grades 3-6 • Prentice Hall Regents © by Judie Haynes and Elizabeth Claire

Instructions: page T48

# Ordinal Numbers

## A. Read the numbers.

| **1st**<br>first | **2nd**<br>second | **3rd**<br>third | **4th**<br>fourth |
|---|---|---|---|
| **5th**<br>fifth | **6th**<br>sixth | **21st**<br>twenty-first | **32nd**<br>thirty-second |

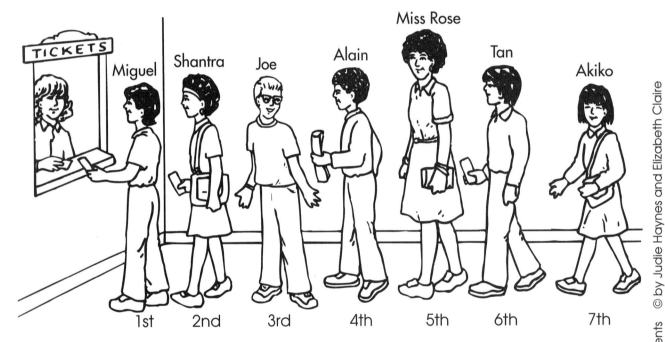

Miguel — 1st | Shantra — 2nd | Joe — 3rd | Alain — 4th | Miss Rose — 5th | Tan — 6th | Akiko — 7th

## B. Write the answers.

1. Who is first? _____

2. Who is second? _____

3. Who is third? _____

4. Who is fifth? _____

5. Who is last? _____

# Draw the Hands on the Clocks

It's two o'clock.

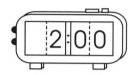

It's two-ten.

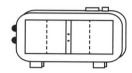

It's two-fifteen.

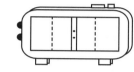

It's two twenty-five.

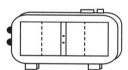

It's two-thirty.

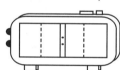

It's two-forty.

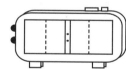

It's two forty-five.

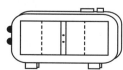

It's two fifty-nine.

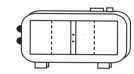

It's three o'clock.

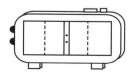

Newcomer Program, Grades 3-6 • Prentice Hall Regents    © by Judie Haynes and Elizabeth Claire

Instructions: page T49

# What Time Is It?

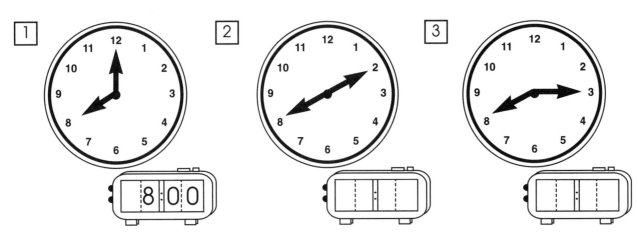

1. __It's eight o'clock.__ _____
2. _____
3. _____

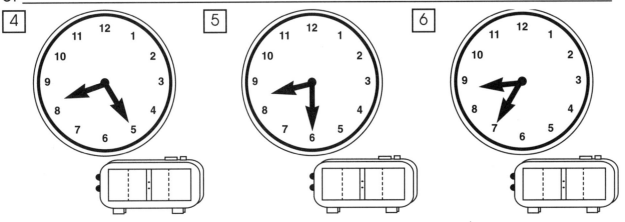

4. _____
5. _____
6. _____

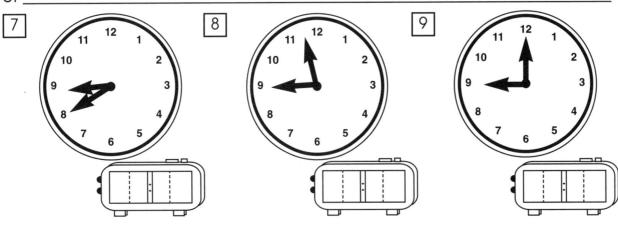

7. _____
8. _____
9. _____

Newcomer Program, Grades 3-6 • Prentice Hall Regents    © by Judie Haynes and Elizabeth Claire

Name _____

Date _____

# Calendar

| | Sunday | Monday | Tuesday | Wednesday | Thursday | Friday | Saturday |
|---|---|---|---|---|---|---|---|
| | | | | | | | |
| | | | | | | | |
| | | | | | | | |
| | | | | | | | |
| | | | | | | | |

Newcomer Program, Grades 3-6 • Prentice Hall Regents    © by Judie Haynes and Elizabeth Claire

Instructions: page T49

# What Day Is It?

| Monday | Tuesday | Wednesday | Thursday |
|---|---|---|---|
| Friday | Saturday | Sunday | |

## A. Unscramble the names of the days.

1. eyaustd _____     5. drifya _____

2. nmyoda _____     6. trasydau _____

3. hdyuastr _____     7. ysnuda _____

4. ddeweynas _____

## B. Write the answers.

1. What days of the week do you go to school? _____

_____

2. What day of the week is today? _____

3. What day of the week was yesterday? _____

4. What day of the week will tomorrow be? _____

5. What days of the week don't you go to school? _____

_____

6. What is your favorite day of the week? Why? _____

_____

Newcomer Program, Grades 3-6 • Prentice Hall Regents   © by Judie Haynes and Elizabeth Claire

# Months of the Year Cards

January

February

March

April

May

June

July

August

September

October

November

December

Instructions: page T50

# What Month Is It?

| January | February | March | April |
|---------|----------|-------|-------|
| May | June | July | August |
| September | October | November | December |

## A. Unscramble the names of the months.

1. yjul _____
2. cramh _____
3. vroeebmn _____
4. njeu _____
5. yam _____
6. pesrebmet _____

7. gtsuua _____
8. plira _____
9. rrfyeaub _____
10. oroebtc _____
11. yuarnaj _____
12. becdemre _____

## B. Write your answers.

1. In which month were you born? _____

2. Which month is your favorite? Why? _____

_____

_____

_____

_____

_____

Newcomer Program, Grades 3-6 • Prentice Hall Regents   © by Judie Haynes and Elizabeth Claire

# Birthday Survey – 1

**Ask, "When is your birthday?" Write each person's name where it belongs on the chart.**

| January | February | March | April | May | June |
|---|---|---|---|---|---|
|  |  |  |  |  |  |
|  |  |  |  |  |  |
|  |  |  |  |  |  |
|  |  |  |  |  |  |
|  |  |  |  |  |  |
|  |  |  |  |  |  |

| July | August | September | October | November | December |
|---|---|---|---|---|---|
|  |  |  |  |  |  |
|  |  |  |  |  |  |
|  |  |  |  |  |  |
|  |  |  |  |  |  |
|  |  |  |  |  |  |
|  |  |  |  |  |  |

Newcomer Program, Grades 3-6 • Prentice Hall Regents    © by Judie Haynes and Elizabeth Claire

Instructions: page T50

# Birthday Survey – 2

## Use your survey to answer the questions.

1. In which month is your birthday? _____

2. Which month has the most birthdays? _____

3. Which month has the fewest birthdays? _____

4. In which month is your teacher's birthday? _____

5. Are there more birthdays in the first six months or in the last six months of the year? _____

   _____

6. How many students have birthdays in January?

   _____

7. How many students have birthdays in April?

   _____

8. How many students have birthdays in September?

   _____

9. How many students have birthdays during the winter?

   _____

10. How many students have birthdays during the summer vacation? _____

11. Are there more birthdays in September or in January?

    _____

12. Are there more birthdays in April or in June?

    _____

Newcomer Program, Grades 3-6 • Prentice Hall Regents    © by Judie Haynes and Elizabeth Claire

# Color Words – 1

## A. Color the crayons. Add and label other colors.

 red

 orange

 yellow

 green

 blue

 _____

 red

 orange

 yellow

 green

 blue

 _____

## B. Use a color word to finish each sentence.

1. Snowflakes ❄❄❄ are _____.

2. Grapes 🍇 are _____.

3. The sun ☀ is _____.

4. Trees 🌳🌲 are _____.

5. Cherries 🍒 are _____.

6. Carrots 🥕 are _____.

7. Spiders 🕷🕷 are _____.

8. My favorite color is _____.

Instructions: page T50

# Color Words – 2

## A. Color the circles.

(1) blue        (4) yellow        (7) black

(2) red         (5) brown         (8) purple

(3) green       (6) orange        (9) pink

## B. Use the numbers to color the picture.

# Clothing Cards – 1

| | | | |
|---|---|---|---|
| umbrella | hat | bathing suit | sunglasses |
| blouse | sweatshirt | backpack | tie |
| coat | scarf | sundress | necklace |
| stockings | socks | pajamas | suit |
| mittens | shorts | ring | |

Instructions: page T51

# Clothing Cards – 2

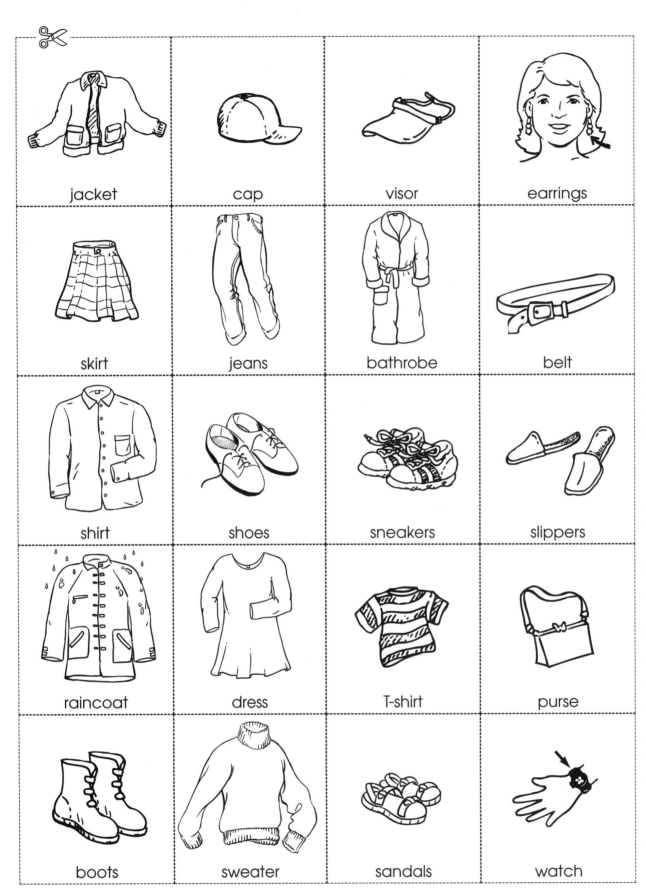

| | | | |
|---|---|---|---|
| jacket | cap | visor | earrings |
| skirt | jeans | bathrobe | belt |
| shirt | shoes | sneakers | slippers |
| raincoat | dress | T-shirt | purse |
| boots | sweater | sandals | watch |

Newcomer Program, Grades 3-6 • Prentice Hall Regents   © by Judie Haynes and Elizabeth Claire

# Game Board

**Place 24 cards on the board.  Use any order you like.**

| | | | | |
|---|---|---|---|---|
| | | | | |
| | | | | |
| | | FREE | | |
| | | | | |
| | | | | |

Newcomer Program, Grades 3-6 • Prentice Hall Regents    © by Judie Haynes and Elizabeth Claire

Instructions: page T51

# Pack for a Trip

## Where do you want go?
## Show what you need to pack.

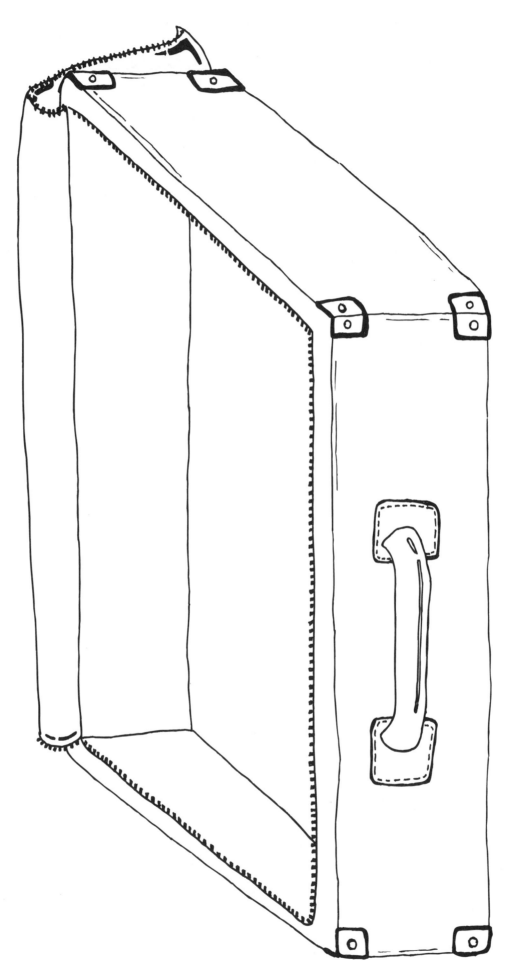

# What Will You Wear? – 1

**Draw yourself. Label what you are wearing.**

I am playing outside. It is snowing.

I am at the park. It is sunny.

# What Will You Wear? – 2

**Draw yourself. Label what you are wearing.**

I am walking to school. It is raining.

I am at the beach. It is sunny.

Newcomer Program, Grades 3-6 • Prentice Hall Regents  © by Judie Haynes and Elizabeth Claire

# Clothing Survey

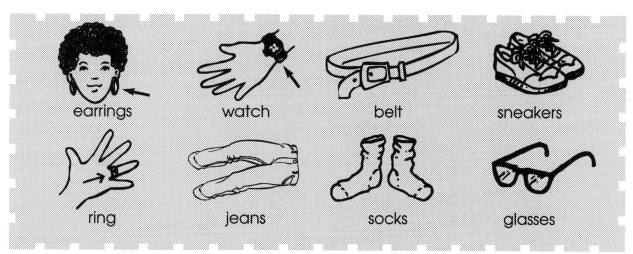

earrings    watch    belt    sneakers

ring    jeans    socks    glasses

## Write sentences about your classmates.

1. Find someone who is wearing earrings.
   **Mary is wearing earrings.** _____

2. Find someone who is wearing a belt.
   _____

3. Find someone who is wearing a ring.
   _____

4. Find someone who is wearing a watch.
   _____

5. Find someone who isn't wearing jeans.
   _____

6. Find someone who isn't wearing white socks.
   _____

7. Find someone who isn't wearing glasses.
   _____

8. Find someone who isn't wearing sneakers.
   _____

# Food Cards – 1

| | | | |
|---|---|---|---|
| banana | apple | orange | water |
| grapes | pear | strawberries | rice |
| carrot | peas | green beans | bread |
| corn | lettuce | beans | tomato |
| sandwich | fish | potato | milk |
| chicken | hamburger | eggs | tea |

Newcomer Program, Grades 3-6 • Prentice Hall Regents    © by Judie Haynes and Elizabeth Claire

# Food Cards – 2

| | | | |
|---|---|---|---|
| coffee | lemonade | onion | salad |
| soup | cheese | spaghetti | pizza |
| french fries | watermelon | peppers | juice |
| popcorn | hot dog | broccoli | mushrooms |

Instructions: page T53

# My Feelings about Foods

| Things I Love! ☺ | Things I Like ☺ | Things I Don't Like ☹ | Things I Hate! ☹ |
|---|---|---|---|
| | | | |

Newcomer Program, Grades 3-6 • Prentice Hall Regents   © by Judie Haynes and Elizabeth Claire

# Plan a Meal

## Label each item.

knife    plate    cup    fork    bowl    saucer    spoon    napkin    glass

# Favorite Fruit Survey – 1

Ask, "What is your favorite fruit?" Write each person's name beside his or her favorite fruit.

| | | | |
|---|---|---|---|
| apples | bananas | cherries | oranges |
| pears | grapes | strawberries | pineapples |
| apricots | mangoes | papayas | blueberries |
| watermelon | grapefruit | peaches | plums |
| nuts | figs | kiwi | melon |

Newcomer Program, Grades 3-6 • Prentice Hall Regents    © by Judie Haynes and Elizabeth Claire

# Favorite Fruit Survey – 2

## A. Show how well your class likes these fruits.

| Number of Students | 1 | 2 | 3 | 4 | 5 | 6 | 7 | 8 | 9 | 10 | 11 | 12 |
|---|---|---|---|---|---|---|---|---|---|---|---|---|
| apples | | | | | | | | | | | | |
| apricots | | | | | | | | | | | | |
| bananas | | | | | | | | | | | | |
| blueberries | | | | | | | | | | | | |
| cherries | | | | | | | | | | | | |
| figs | | | | | | | | | | | | |
| grapefruit | | | | | | | | | | | | |
| grapes | | | | | | | | | | | | |
| kiwi | | | | | | | | | | | | |
| mangoes | | | | | | | | | | | | |
| melon | | | | | | | | | | | | |
| nuts | | | | | | | | | | | | |
| oranges | | | | | | | | | | | | |
| papayas | | | | | | | | | | | | |
| peaches | | | | | | | | | | | | |
| pears | | | | | | | | | | | | |
| pineapples | | | | | | | | | | | | |
| plums | | | | | | | | | | | | |
| strawberries | | | | | | | | | | | | |
| watermelon | | | | | | | | | | | | |

## B. Use your graph to find answers.

1. What fruit is liked most? _____

2. What fruit is liked least? _____

3. How many people like your favorite fruit? _____

Name _____  Date _____

# Where Is It?

**Cut out the birds. Glue each bird in the correct place.**

The bird is **on** the birdhouse.

The bird is **in** the birdhouse.

The bird is **under** the birdhouse.

The bird is **next to** the birdhouse.

The bird is **behind** the birdhouse.

The bird is **between** the birdhouse and the tree.

# Where Will You Draw It?

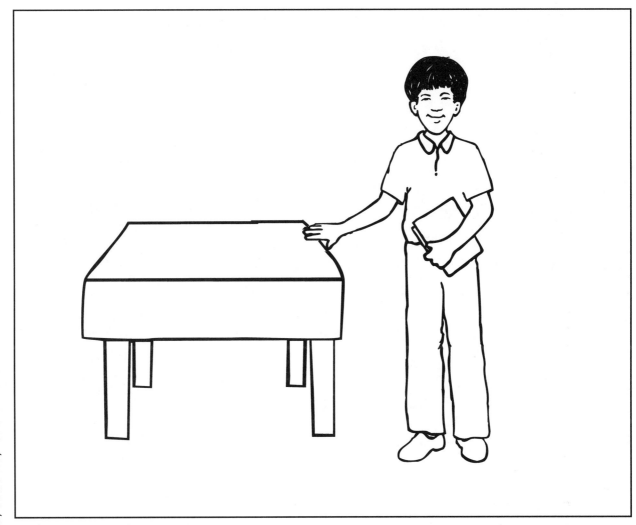

## Finish the picture.

1. Draw a hat on the boy.

2. Draw a wastebasket behind the boy.

3. Draw a book on the table.

4. Draw a cup next to the book.

5. Draw a pencil in the cup.

6. Draw a cat between the boy and the table.

7. Draw a box in the wastebasket.

8. Draw a ball under the table.

# Verb Cards

| | | | |
|---|---|---|---|
| walk | run | jump | write |
| climb | talk | eat | listen |
| drink | sleep | sit | open |
| play | read | point | sing |
| stand | look | draw | smile |

Newcomer Program , Grades, 3-6 • Prentice Hall Regents    © by Judie Haynes and Elizabeth Claire

Name _____ Date _____

# Action Words

**A. Verbs are things you can do. Act out these verbs with a friend.**

| drink | sit | write | jump | open | talk |
| listen | stand | play | sleep | read | draw |

**B. Write the correct verb in each sentence.**

1. I _r_ __ __ __ a book.

2. I __ __ __ __ __ __ to the teacher.

3. I __ __ __ __ __ milk.

4. I __ __ __ in the chair.

5. I __ __ __ __ ball.

6. I __ __ __ __ my backpack.

7. I __ __ __ __ __ in bed.

8. I __ __ __ __ up and down.

9. I __ __ __ __ __ my name.

10. I __ __ __ __ __ in line.

11. I __ __ __ __ my pictures.

12. I __ __ __ __ on the telephone.

**C. Draw pictures for two of the sentences.**

Newcomer Program, Grades 3-6 • Prentice Hall Regents    © by Judie Haynes and Elizabeth Claire

Instructions: page T55

# Noun or Verb?

## Sort these words. Write them in the correct list.

| **Verb**<br>(something you do) | | **Noun**<br>(a person, place, or thing) |
|---|---|---|
| 1. _____ | jacket | 1. _____ |
| | pencil | |
| | point | |
| 2. _____ | jeans | 2. _____ |
| | sleep | |
| 3. _____ | climb | 3. _____ |
| | crayons | |
| | draw | |
| 4. _____ | sweater | 4. _____ |
| | talk | |
| 5. _____ | paper | 5. _____ |
| | write | |
| 6. _____ | shirt | 6. _____ |
| | socks | |
| | listen | |
| 7. _____ | sneakers | 7. _____ |
| | open | |
| 8. _____ | sing | 8. _____ |
| | sleep | |
| 9. _____ | shoes | 9. _____ |
| | backpack | |
| 10. _____ | | 10. _____ |

Newcomer Program, Grades 3-6 • Prentice Hall Regents    © by Judie Haynes and Elizabeth Claire

# More Than One

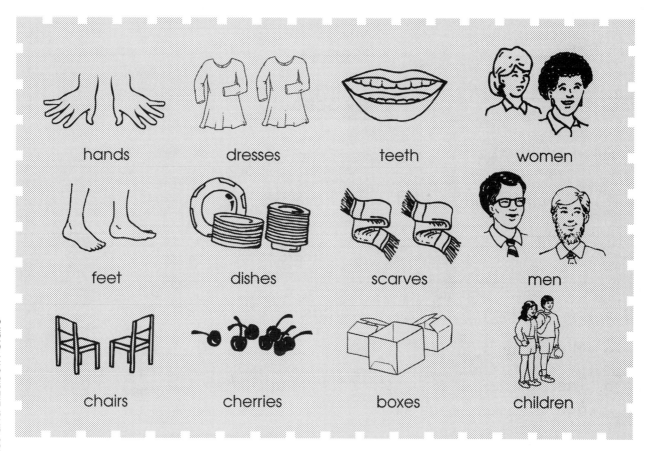

hands       dresses       teeth       women

feet       dishes       scarves       men

chairs       cherries       boxes       children

## Write the words for more than one.

1. foot _____
2. scarf _____
3. chair _____
4. woman _____
5. dress _____
6. hand _____

7. man _____
8. tooth _____
9. child _____
10. cherry _____
11. dish _____
12. box _____

Instructions: page T55

## My School

Fill in the blanks.

1. The name of my school is _____ .

2. It is at _____ .
   (street)
   in _____ , _____ .
   (town) (state)

3. I am in the _____ grade.

4. My teacher's name is _____ .

5. There are _____ students in my class, _____ boys
   and _____ girls.

6. My class is in room number _____ . It is on the _____
   floor.

7. The principal of the school is _____ .

8. I go to these other classes.

| Class | Teacher |
| --- | --- |
| _____ | _____ |
| _____ | _____ |
| _____ | _____ |
| _____ | _____ |
| _____ | _____ |

Newcomer Program, Grades 3-6 • Prentice Hall Regents   © by Judie Haynes and Elizabeth Claire

# School Activity Cards

Reading

Math

Music

Science

Art

Social Studies

Gym

Lunch

ESL

Library

Computer Class

Writing

Instructions: page T56

# Daily Schedule

| Morning | | Afternoon | |
|---|---|---|---|
| Time | Activity | Time | Activity |
| | | | |
| | | | |
| | | | |
| | | | |

Newcomer Program, Grades 3–6 • Prentice Hall Regents   © by Judie Haynes and Elizabeth Claire

Name _____

Date _____

# In the Classroom

# In the Classroom – 1

## A. Look, listen, and read.

This is a classroom. The teacher's name is Miss Rose. Miss Rose is teaching math now. Tan, Po Wen, and Mei are listening. Mei doesn't understand. She is raising her hand. She wants to ask a question. Alain is writing on the chalkboard. Shantra is copying the words. Miguel is reading a book. Nadia is sharpening a pencil. Akiko and Carmen are looking at the fish. Palo is coming in the door. Jennifer and Joe are talking.

## B. Match. Write the letters.

_____ 1.  Miss Rose                    a.  is reading a book.

_____ 2.  Tan, Po Wen and Mei          b.  is teaching math.

_____ 3.  Mei                          c.  are listening.

_____ 4.  Alain                        d.  doesn't understand.

_____ 5.  Shantra                      e.  is writing on the chalkboard.

_____ 6.  Miguel                       f.  is looking at the fish.

_____ 7.  Nadia                        g.  is coming in the door.

_____ 8.  Akiko                        h.  are talking.

_____ 9.  Palo                         i.  is sharpening a pencil.

_____10.  Jennifer and Joe             j.  is copying the words.

## C. Copy the sentences on another sheet of paper.

Newcomer Program, Grades 3-6 • Prentice Hall Regents    © by Judie Haynes and Elizabeth Claire

# In the Classroom – 2

## A. Match. Write the letters.

_____ 1.   door

_____ 2.   book

_____ 3.   pencil

_____ 4.   chalkboard

## B. Listen, read, and write.

| teaching | ask | pencil | chalkboard |
| listening | is | name | understand |
| looking | and | book | hand |

This is a classroom. The teacher's _____ is

Miss Rose. Miss Rose is _____ math now. Tan,

Po Wen, and Mei are _____. Mei doesn't

_____. She is raising her _____.

She wants to _____ a question. Alain is writing

on the _____. Shantra _____

copying the words. Miguel is reading a _____.

Nadia is sharpening a _____. Akiko and

Carmen are _____ at the fish. Palo is coming in

the door. Jennifer _____ Joe are talking.

Instructions: pages T57, T58

# In the Classroom – 3

## A. Color these items in the picture on page 71.

1. Miss Rose's dress is red.

2. The fish is yellow.

3. Palo's shirt is blue.

4. Palo's pants are black.

5. Akiko's blouse is green.

6. Jennifer's skirt is purple.

7. Alain's shoes are black.

8. Carmen's dress is orange.

## B. Color the rest of the picture.

## C. Write five sentences about the picture.

_____

_____

_____

_____

_____

_____

_____

_____

_____

_____

_____

_____

Newcomer Program, Grades 3-6 • Prentice Hall Regents    © by Judie Haynes and Elizabeth Claire

# In the Classroom – 4

## Draw a picture for each sentence.

1

A girl is raising her hand.

2

A boy is reading a book.

3

Two children are talking.

4

A boy is sharpening a pencil.

5

A girl is writing on the chalkboard.

6

Three boys are looking at the fish.

# In the Classroom – 5

**Draw a picture for each word.**

| 1 | 2 | 3 |
|---|---|---|
| desk | pencil sharpener | chair |

| 4 | 5 | 6 |
|---|---|---|
| flag | chalkboard | clock |

| 7 | 8 | 9 |
|---|---|---|
| book | wastebasket | table |

| 10 | 11 | 12 |
|---|---|---|
| _____ | _____ | _____ |

Newcomer Program, Grades 3-6 • Prentice Hall Regents    © by Judie Haynes and Elizabeth Claire

# In the Bathroom

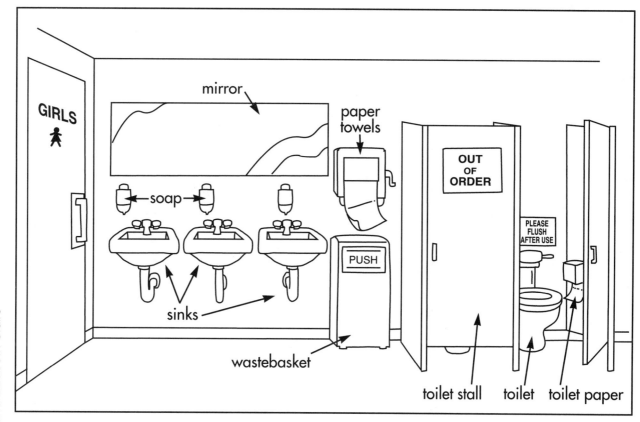

## Look at the picture.  Write the correct words in the sentences.

1. This is the girl's _____.

2. The door to the _____ stall is open.

3. The _____is next to the toilet.

4. Use _____ to wash your hands.

5. There are three _____ in the girl's bathroom.

6. Throw wet paper towels in the _____.

7. You can look in the _____ to comb your hair.

Instructions: pages T57, T59

# In Music Class

America the Beautiful

O beautiful
For spacious skies
For amber waves of grain
For purple mountains
majesty
Above the fruited plains

Mr. Brooks

Miguel

Akiko

Alain

Jennifer

Palo

Joe

Nadia

Newcomer Program, Grades 3-6 • Prentice Hall Regents   © by Judie Haynes and Elizabeth Claire

# In Music Class – 1

## A. Look, listen, and read.

This is a music class. The teacher's name is Mr. Brooks. Mr. Brooks is playing the piano. Akiko and Miguel are singing. Jennifer is playing the drums. Joe is playing the flute. Nadia and Palo are clapping their hands. The words to the song are on the chalkboard. Alain is copying the words.

## B. Check (✔) the correct answer.

|  | Yes | No |
|---|---|---|
| 1. This is a music class. | | |
| 2. The teacher's name is Mrs. Brooks. | | |
| 3. Mr. Brooks is playing the flute. | | |
| 4. Some children are playing the piano. | | |
| 5. Jennifer is playing the drums. | | |
| 6. Joe is singing. | | |
| 7. Nadia and Palo are clapping their hands. | | |
| 8. The song is "America the Beautiful." | | |
| 9. Alain is copying the words. | | |
| 10. Akiko is not in music class. | | |

Newcomer Program, Grades 3-6 • Prentice Hall Regents   © by Judie Haynes and Elizabeth Claire

Instructions: page T57

# In Music Class – 2

## A. Match. Write the letters.

_____ 1.  piano

_____ 2.  drum

_____ 3.  flute

_____ 4.  song

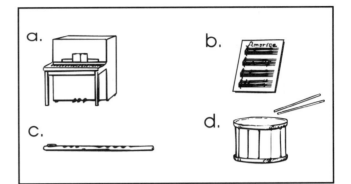

## B. Listen, read, and write.

| | | |
|---|---|---|
| chalkboard | Alain | Mr. |
| singing | music | is |
| playing | hands | flute |

This is a _____ class. The teacher's name

is _____ Brooks. Mr. Brooks is _____

the piano. Akiko and Miguel are _____.

Jennifer _____ playing the drums. Joe is

playing the _____. Nadia and Palo are

clapping their _____. The words to the song

are on the _____. _____ is

copying the words.

Newcomer Program, Grades 3-6 • Prentice Hall Regents   © by Judie Haynes and Elizabeth Claire

# In Music Class – 3

## Find and circle these words in the puzzle.

| | | | | |
|---|---|---|---|---|
| America | copy | ~~hands~~ | words | singing |
| chalkboard | drum | music | piano | sitting |
| clapping | song | name | flute | standing |
| class | | playing | | teacher |

```
H  U  K  C  V  W  P  K  K  D  R  U  M  Q
C  R  N  H  H  C  A  L  N  S  L  A  Z  P
O  J  Q  E  A  A  P  M  A  S  J  P  O  S
G  S  T  T  H  N  L  M  E  Y  O  A  B  I
H  S  I  E  Z  T  D  K  I  R  I  N  Y  N
B  C  T  T  A  Q  T  S  B  S  I  N  G  G
P  L  U  A  T  C  W  C  M  O  T  C  G  I
R  A  O  G  N  I  H  O  C  U  A  Y  A  N
F  P  Q  Q  Z  D  N  E  R  L  S  R  F  G
L  P  F  S  L  G  I  G  R  D  A  I  D  D
U  I  T  S  Y  M  R  N  V  E  S  S  C  N
T  N  B  U  N  T  T  S  G  D  X  Q  S  H
E  G  L  P  I  A  N  O  C  O  P  Y  L  O
X  L  D  B  N  A  M  E  M  Y  J  A  H  V
```

Instructions: pages T57, T58, T71

# In Music Class – 4

## Draw a picture for each sentence.

| | |
|---|---|
| **1** <br><br><br><br><br><br> A girl is playing the flute. | **2** <br><br><br><br><br><br> Two children are singing. |
| **3** <br><br><br><br><br><br> A boy is clapping his hands. | **4** <br><br><br><br><br><br> A girl is copying the words. |
| **5** <br><br><br><br><br><br> A teacher is playing the drums. | **6** <br><br><br><br><br><br> The words are on the chalkboard. |

Newcomer Program, Grades 3-6 • Prentice Hall Regents   © by Judie Haynes and Elizabeth Claire

# In Art Class

Mr. Nichols

Akiko

Jennifer

Carmen

Joe

Alain

Miguel

Palo

Shantra

Nadia

# In Art Class – 1

## A. Look, Listen, and Read.

This is an art class. The art teacher's name is Mr. Nichols. Mr. Nichols is showing the class how to make kites. Akiko is measuring her paper. Jennifer is cutting. Miguel is drawing a face on his kite. Carmen is coloring her kite. Joe is pasting. Nadia and Alain are painting dragons on their kites. Shantra is tying a tail on her kite. Palo is flying his kite outside.

## B. Check (✔) the correct answer.

| | Yes | No |
|---|---|---|
| 1. This is an art class. | | |
| 2. The teacher's name is Miss Nichols. | | |
| 3. Mr. Nichols is showing the class how to make cookies. | | |
| 4. Akiko is measuring her paper. | | |
| 5. Miguel is drawing a dragon on his kite. | | |
| 6. Akiko is coloring her kite. | | |
| 7. Joe is pasting. | | |
| 8. Nadia and Shantra are painting dragons on their kites. | | |
| 9. Jennifer is tying a tail on her kite. | | |
| 10. Palo and Tan are flying their kites outside. | | |

Newcomer Program, Grades 3-6 • Prentice Hall Regents    © by Judie Haynes and Elizabeth Claire

# In Art Class – 2

## A. Match. Write the letters.

_____ 1.  measure

_____ 2.  draw

_____ 3.  paint

_____ 4.  color

_____ 5.  cut

_____ 6.  tie

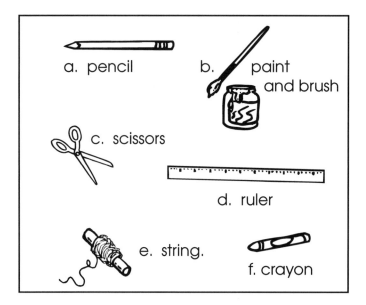

a. pencil  b.  paint and brush

c. scissors

d. ruler

e. string.  f. crayon

## B. Listen, read, and write.

| kite | Akiko | name | class | is | coloring |
|------|-------|------|-------|-----|----------|
| cutting | their | outside | are | her | face |

This is an art _____. The teacher's

_____ is Mr. Nichols. Mr. Nichols is showing the class

how to make _____. _____ is

measuring her paper. Jennifer is _____. Miguel is

drawing a _____ on his kite. Carmen is

_____ her kite. Joe _____ pasting.

Nadia and Alain _____ painting dragons on

_____ kites. Shantra is tying a tail on

_____ kite. Palo is flying his kite _____.

Instructions: pages T57, T58

# In Art Class – 3

**Draw a picture for each sentence.**

| 1 | 2 |
|---|---|
| A girl is cutting paper. | There is a face on the kite. |

| 3 | 4 |
|---|---|
| A boy is measuring his paper. | The kite has a long tail. |

5

A girl is flying a kite.

Newcomer Program, Grades 3-6 • Prentice Hall Regents     © by Judie Haynes and Elizabeth Claire

Name _____

Date _____

# In Gym Class

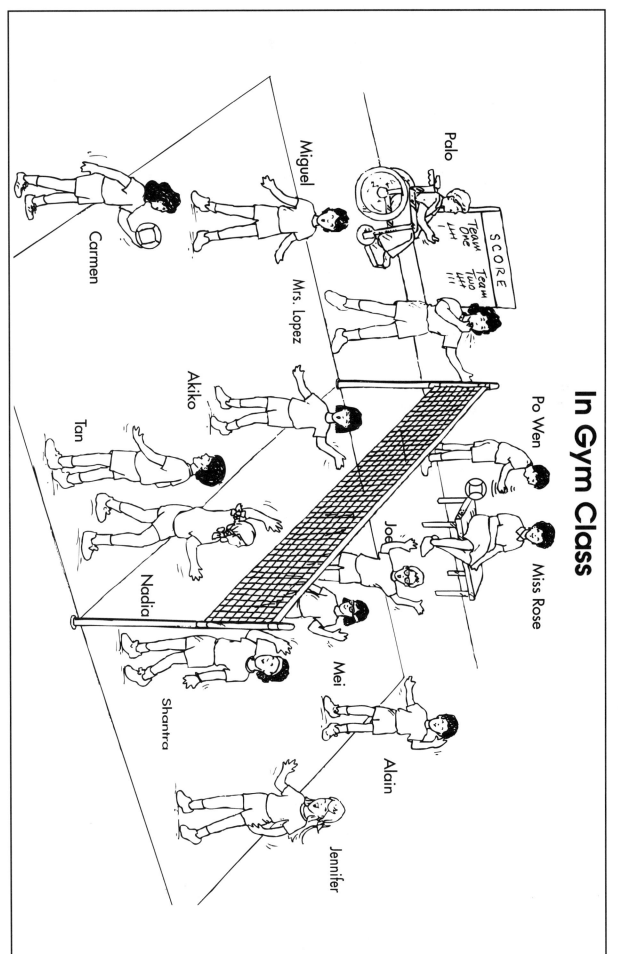

Palo, Miguel, Mrs. Lopez, Carmen, Akiko, Tan, Nadia, Shantra, Po Wen, Joe, Miss Rose, Mei, Alain, Jennifer

Newcomer Program, Grades 3–6 • Prentice Hall Regents   © by Judie Haynes and Elizabeth Claire

Instructions: page T57

Name _____ Date _____

# In Gym Class – 1

## A. Look, listen, and read.

   This is a gym class. The students are playing
volleyball. Nadia, Carmen, Akiko, Tan and Miguel are
on Team One. Alain, Shantra, Mei, Jennifer, and Joe are
on Team Two. The gym teacher's name is Mrs. Lopez.
Mrs. Lopez is blowing her whistle. Carmen is serving the
ball. She wants the ball to go over the net. Miss Rose is
sitting on a bench. She is watching the game. Po Wen is
bouncing a ball. Palo is keeping score. Team Two is
winning. Team One is losing.

## B. Check (✔) the correct answer.

|  | Yes | No |
|---|---|---|
| 1. This is a gym class. | | |
| 2. The students are playing basketball. | | |
| 3. The gym teacher's name is Miss Rose. | | |
| 4. Mrs. Lopez is carrying her whistle. | | |
| 5. Carmen is serving the ball. | | |
| 6. Carmen wants the ball to go under the net. | | |
| 7. Miss Rose is watching the game. | | |
| 8. Po Wen is bouncing a ball. | | |
| 9. Palo is keeping score. | | |
| 10. Team Two is losing. | | |

Newcomer Program, Grades 3-6 • Prentice Hall Regents   © by Judie Haynes and Elizabeth Claire

# In Gym Class – 2

## A. Match. Write the letters.

_____ 1. volleyball

_____ 2. whistle

_____ 3. score

_____ 4. net

_____ 5. bench

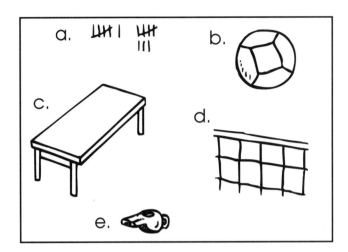

## B. Listen, read, and write.

| over | bench | winning | volleyball | losing | one |
|------|-------|---------|------------|--------|-----|
| gym | Team | watching | bouncing | score | her |

This is a _____ class. The students are playing

_____. Nadia, Carmen, Akiko, Tan, and Miguel are

on Team _____. Alain, Shantra, Mei, Jennifer, and

Joe are on _____ Two. The gym teacher's name is

Mrs. Lopez. Mrs. Lopez is blowing _____ whistle.

Carmen is serving the ball. She wants the ball to go

_____ the net. Miss Rose is sitting on a

_____. She is _____ the game. Po

Wen is _____ a ball. Palo is keeping

_____. Team Two is _____. Team

One is _____.

 Instructions: pages T57, T58

# In Gym Class – 3

## Draw a picture for each sentence.

| 1 | 2 |
|---|---|
| A teacher is blowing a whistle. | A girl is serving the ball. |

| 3 | 4 |
|---|---|
| A boy is keeping score. | The score is eight to six. |

| 5 | 6 |
|---|---|
| A boy is sitting on a bench. | A ball is going over the net. |

Newcomer Program, Grades 3–6 • Prentice Hall Regents    © by Judie Haynes and Elizabeth Claire

# In the Lunchroom

CAFETERIA

Mrs. Heinke

Po Wen

Mei

Ms. Worth

Joe

Nadia

Jennifer

Miguel

Carmen

Shantra

Alain

Palo

# In the Lunchroom – 1

## A. Look, listen, and read.

This is a school lunchroom. Po Wen and Mei are standing in line. They are getting a school lunch. Nadia is carrying a tray to the table. Some students are at the table. Joe, Miguel, and Jennifer brought their lunches from home. Joe is opening his lunch bag. Miguel is eating a sandwich. He is talking to Joe. Jennifer is drinking juice. Palo is laughing with Carmen. Alain is doing homework. Shantra is throwing a banana peel in the garbage.

## B. Check (✔) the correct answer.

| | Yes | No |
|---|---|---|
| 1. Po Wen and Miguel are standing in line. | | |
| 2. Mei is doing her homework. | | |
| 3. Nadia is carrying a tray. | | |
| 4. Jennifer brought her lunch from home. | | |
| 5. Joe is laughing with Carmen. | | |
| 6. Miguel is opening his lunch bag. | | |
| 7. Jennifer is drinking juice. | | |
| 8. Palo is eating a sandwich. | | |
| 9. Alain is getting a school lunch. | | |
| 10. Shantra is throwing a banana peel in the garbage. | | |

Newcomer Program, Grades 3-6 • Prentice Hall Regents   © by Judie Haynes and Elizabeth Claire

# In the Lunchroom – 2

## A. Listen, read, and write.

| | | | | | |
|---|---|---|---|---|---|
| laughing | standing | sandwich | lunch | carrying | opening |
| brought | homework | school | juice | throwing | garbage |

This is a school lunchroom. Po Wen and Mei are

_____ in line. They are getting a school

_____. Nadia is _____ a tray to the

table. Some _____ are at the table. Joe, Miguel,

and Jennifer _____ their lunches from home. Joe is

_____ his lunch bag. Miguel is eating a

_____. He is talking to Joe. Jennifer is drinking

_____. Palo is _____ with Carmen.

Alain is doing _____. Shantra is

_____ a banana peel in the _____.

## B. Match. Write the letters.

_____ 1. Nadia                a. is opening his lunch bag.

_____ 2. Po Wen and Mei       b. is eating a sandwich.

_____ 3. Joe                  c. are standing in line.

_____ 4. Shantra              d. are laughing.

_____ 5. Miguel               e. is drinking juice.

_____ 6. Jennifer             f. is doing homework.

_____ 7. Palo and Carmen      g. is carrying a tray.

_____ 8. Alain                h. is throwing a banana peel in the garbage.

     Instructions: pages T57, T58

# In the Lunchroom – 3

**Draw a picture for each sentence.**

| | |
|---|---|
| 1<br><br><br><br><br><br><br>Two students are standing in line. | 2<br><br><br><br><br><br><br>A girl is drinking juice. |
| 3<br><br><br><br><br><br><br>A girl is carrying a tray. | 4<br><br><br><br><br><br><br>A boy is eating a sandwich. |
| 5<br><br><br><br><br><br><br>A boy is opening his lunch bag. | 6<br><br><br><br><br><br><br>A girl is throwing garbage away. |

Newcomer Program, Grades 3-6 • Prentice Hall Regents   © by Judie Haynes and Elizabeth Claire

# In the Lunchroom – 4

## A. Color these items in the picture on page 91.

1. Po Wen's jeans are blue.

2. Nadia's sweatpants are purple.

3. Mei's bow is pink.

4. Palo's vest is red.

5. Joe's sneakers are white.

6. Carmen's purse is tan.

7. Alain's turtleneck is green.

8. Shantra's headband is orange.

9. Shantra's belt is brown.

10. Jennifer's cardigan is yellow.

11. Po Wen's sweatshirt is gray.

12. Nadia's jacket is black.

## B. Color the rest of the picture.

## C. Write five sentences about the picture.

_____

_____

_____

_____

_____

_____

_____

_____

_____

_____

_____

# In the Lunchroom – 5

## Draw a picture for each word.

| | | |
|---|---|---|
| 1 **tray** | 2 **juice** | 3 **turtleneck** |
| 4 **banana peel** | 5 **vest** | 6 **standing** |
| 7 **laughing** | 8 **cardigan** | 9 **sandwich** |
| 10 **sweatshirt** | 11 **lunch bag** | 12 **sitting** |

Newcomer Program, Grades 3-6 • Prentice Hall Regents    © by Judie Haynes and Elizabeth Claire

# In the Library

# In the Library – 1

## A. Look, listen, and read.

This is the school library. The librarian's name is Mrs. Wallace. Mrs. Wallace is helping Po Wen. He is checking out a book. Joe is returning a book. Akiko and Jennifer are looking at a magazine. Palo and Shantra are listening to a story. They are using a tape recorder and headphones. Nadia is looking up a word in the dictionary. Alain is taking a book from the shelf. Miguel is using the encyclopedia.

## B. Check (✔) the correct answer.

| | Yes | No |
|---|---|---|
| 1. The librarian's name is Mrs. Wallace. | | |
| 2. Mrs. Wallace is reading a book. | | |
| 3. Po Wen is returning a book. | | |
| 4. Alain is checking out a book. | | |
| 5. Akiko is listening to a story. | | |
| 6. Jennifer is looking at a magazine. | | |
| 7. Palo and Shantra are using a tape recorder. | | |
| 8. Nadia is looking up a word in the dictionary. | | |
| 9. Joe is taking a book from the shelf. | | |
| 10. Miguel is using the encyclopedia. | | |

Newcomer Program, Grades 3-6 • Prentice Hall Regents   © by Judie Haynes and Elizabeth Claire

# In the Library – 2

## A. Match. Write the letters.

_____ 1.  headphones

_____ 2.  bookshelf

_____ 3.  encyclopedias

_____ 4.  tape recorder

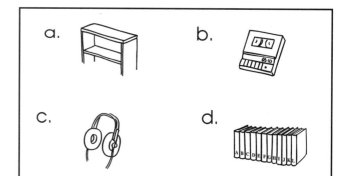

## B. Listen, read, and write.

| shelf | checking out | returning | taking | dictionary |
|---|---|---|---|---|
| helping | headphones | librarian | magazine | encyclopedia |

This is the school library. The _____ 's name is

Mrs. Wallace. Mrs. Wallace is _____ Po Wen. He

is _____ a book. Joe is _____

a book. Akiko and Jennifer are looking at a

_____. Palo and Shantra are listening to a story.

They are using a tape recorder and _____.

Nadia is looking up a word in the _____.

Alain is _____ a book from the

_____. Miguel is using the

_____.

Instructions: pages T57, T58

# In the Library – 3

**Draw a picture for each sentence.**

| | |
|---|---|
| **1**<br><br><br><br><br><br>A girl is reading a magazine. | **2**<br><br><br><br><br>Two students are listening to a story. |
| **3**<br><br><br><br><br>A boy is looking up a word in the dictionary. | **4**<br><br><br><br><br>A girl is taking a book from the shelf. |
| **5**<br><br><br><br><br>A librarian is sitting at her desk. | **6**<br><br><br><br><br>A boy is using headphones. |

# In the Library – 4

**Find and circle these words in the puzzle.**

| | | | | |
|---|---|---|---|---|
| listen | borrow | dictionary | card | encyclopedia |
| magazine | book | library | take | tape recorder |
| headphones | desk | computer | fact | check out |
| bookshelf | return | fiction | read | librarian |

```
B C C H E C K O U T T N O U S F Q
C D G T R F L I B R A R I A N T N
I L M M A G A Z I N E J U N H O F
D D M H A P P W S F F A C T T L F
L I S T E N E W K I I P C R E C E
K C M N N A O R K D C N O H P O Q
E T Z Y X R D U E V T U S T S M R
N I I F R R Y P P C I K P R L P P
I O O O L D O S H R O N E E I U F
C N B N R L N E O O N R U A B T T
H A Q A C R K S B T N D D D R E N
I R C Y V A W X B Y C E K E A R Q
F Y C E T Z R E T U R N S S R R M
M N E F S Y T D W X Y Z K K Y Y R
E R B C A R D G B O O K S M I G R
```

# In the Nurses's Office

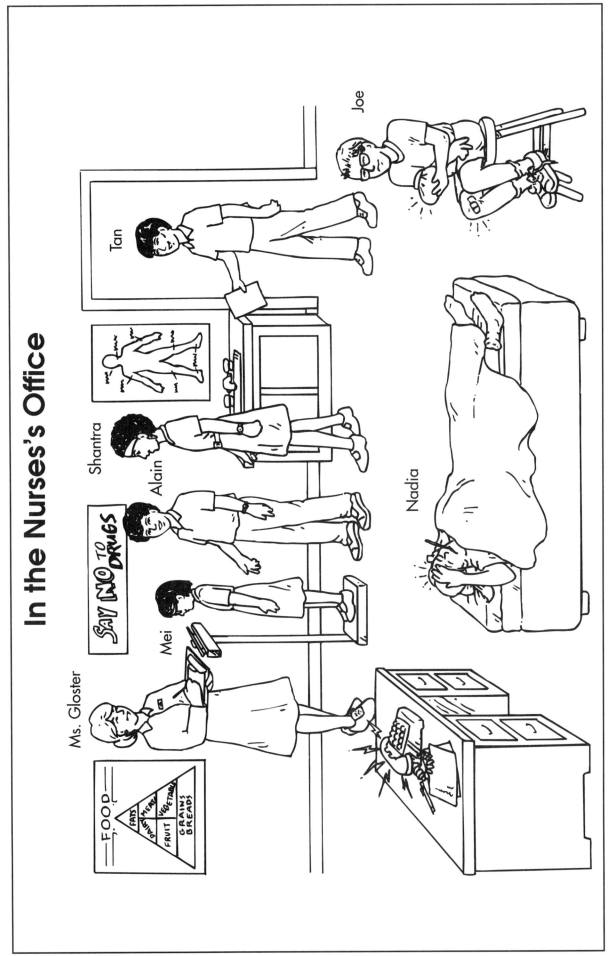

# In the Nurses's Office – 1

## A. Look, listen, and read.

This is the nurse's office. The nurse's name is Ms. Gloster. Mei is on the scale. She is being weighed. Alain and Shantra are waiting for their turn. The telephone is ringing. Nadia is sick. She has a headache. She is lying down. She has a thermometer in her mouth. Joe hurt his elbow and his knee. He has an ice pack on his elbow. He has a Band-Aid on his knee. Tan is bringing a note to Ms. Gloster.

## B. Circle the correct answer.

1. This is a gym class. **Yes** **No**

2. Alain and Shantra are on the scale. **Yes** **No**

3. The nurse's name is Ms. Gloster. **Yes** **No**

4. Alain is lying down. **Yes** **No**

5. Joe has a Band-Aid on his knee. **Yes** **No**

6. Tan has a headache. **Yes** **No**

7. Shantra is bringing a note to Ms. Gloster. **Yes** **No**

8. Nadia has a thermometer in her mouth. **Yes** **No**

9. Mei has an ice pack on her elbow. **Yes** **No**

10. Alain has a headache. **Yes** **No**

Instructions: page T57

# In the Nurses's Office – 2

## A. Listen, read, and write.

| bringing | headache | sick | waiting | nurse |
|----------|----------|------|---------|-------|
| ice pack | thermometer | hurt | Band-Aid | scale |

This is the _____'s office. The nurse's name is Ms. Gloster. Mei is on the _____. She is being weighed. Alain and Shantra are _____ for their turn. The telephone is ringing. Nadia is _____. She has a _____. She is lying down. She has a _____ in her mouth. Joe _____ his elbow and his knee. He has an _____ on his elbow. He has a _____ on his knee. Tan is _____ a note to Ms. Gloster.

## B. Match. Write the letters.

| | |
|---|---|
| _____ 1. Alain | a. has a thermometer in his mouth. |
| _____ 2. Ms. Gloster | b. is bringing a note to the nurse. |
| _____ 3. Tan | c. is waiting to be weighed. |
| _____ 4. Joe | d. has an ice pack on his elbow. |
| _____ 5. Nadia | e. is the school nurse. |

Newcomer Program, Grades 3-6 • Prentice Hall Regents   © by Judie Haynes and Elizabeth Claire

# In the Nurses's Office – 3

## Draw a picture for each sentence.

| 1 | 2 |
|---|---|
| A nurse is weighing a girl. | The telephone is ringing. |

| 3 | 4 |
|---|---|
| A boy has an ice pack on his elbow. | A girl has a Band-Aid on her knee. |

| 5 | 6 |
|---|---|
| A girl is lying down. | A boy is bringing a note to his teacher. |

Instructions: pages T57, T58

# In the Nurses's Office – 4

## Match. Draw lines. Then complete the crossword puzzle.

| ACROSS | | DOWN |
|---|---|---|

**ACROSS**

3.

5. 6.

7.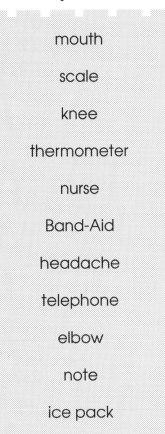

mouth

scale

knee

thermometer

nurse

Band-Aid

headache

telephone

elbow

note

ice pack

8.

9.

**DOWN**

1.

2.

3

4.

5.

Newcomer Program, Grades 3-6 • Prentice Hall Regents    © by Judie Haynes and Elizabeth Claire

# In Science Class

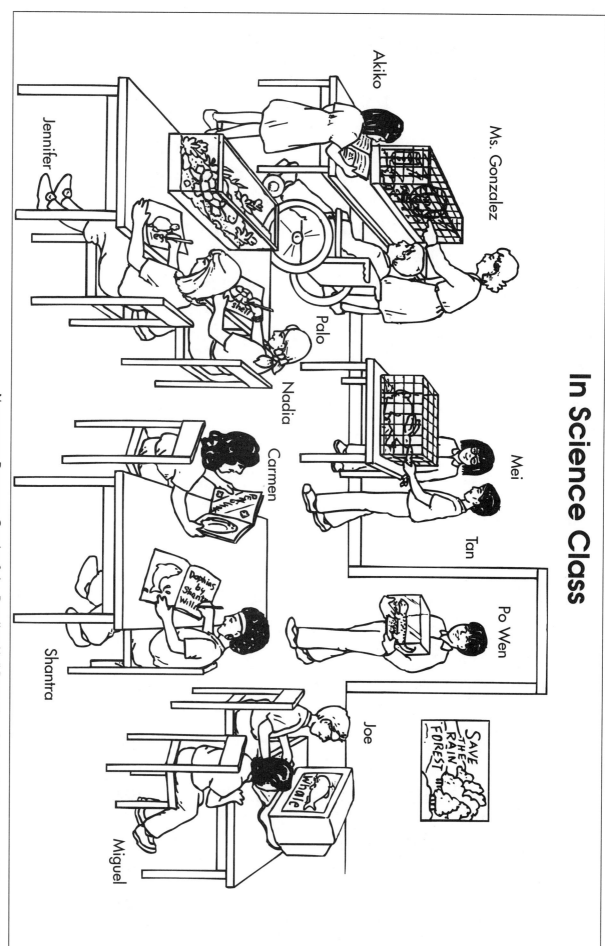

Akiko

Ms. Gonzalez

Jennifer

Palo

Nadia

Mei

Carmen

Tan

Po Wen

Shantra

Joe

Miguel

SAVE THE RAIN FOREST

Whale

Name _____   Date _____

# In Science Class – 1

## A. Look, listen, and read.

This is science class. The class is studying animals. The science teacher's name is Ms. Gonzalez. Palo and Akiko are observing white mice. Tan and Mei are feeding a rabbit. The rabbit is in a cage. Joe and Miguel are at the computer. They are studying whales. A turtle is in the terrarium. Jennifer and Nadia are drawing and labeling pictures of the turtle. Carmen is reading a book about penguins. Shantra is writing a report about dolphins. Po Wen is bringing his iguana to class.

## B. Circle the correct answer.

1. Carmen is reading a book about rabbits.    **Yes    No**

2. There are white mice in the terrarium.    **Yes    No**

3. Joe and Miguel are at the computer.    **Yes    No**

4. The penguin is in a cage.    **Yes    No**

5. Palo is bringing his iguana to class.    **Yes    No**

6. Shantra is writing a report about dolphins.    **Yes    No**

7. Jennifer and Nadia are labeling pictures.    **Yes    No**

8. Ms. Gonzalez is feeding a turtle.    **Yes    No**

9. Akiko is observing white mice.    **Yes    No**

Newcomer Program, Grades 3-6 • Prentice Hall Regents  © by Judie Haynes and Elizabeth Claire

# In Science Class – 2

## Listen, read, and write.

| studying | iguana | observing | mice | report |
|----------|--------|-----------|------|--------|
| penguins | labeling | whales | turtle | dolphins |
| computer | feeding | terrarium | cage | drawing |

This is a science class. The class is _____

animals. The Science teacher's name is Ms. Gonzalez. Palo and

Akiko are _____ white _____.

Tan and Mei are _____ a rabbit. The rabbit

is in a _____. Joe and Miguel are at the

_____. They are studying

_____. A _____ is in the

_____. Jennifer and Nadia are

_____ and _____ pictures of

the turtle. Carmen is reading a book about

_____. Shantra is writing a

_____ about _____.

Po Wen is bringing his _____ to class.

Newcomer Program, Grades 3-6 • Prentice Hall Regents    © by Judie Haynes and Elizabeth Claire

Instructions: pages T57, T58

# In Science Class – 3

## Draw a picture for each sentence.

| | |
|---|---|
| 1<br><br><br><br>White mice are in a cage. | 2<br><br><br><br>A girl is feeding a rabbit. |
| 3<br><br><br><br>A turtle is in a terrarium. | 4<br><br><br><br>A boy is at a computer. |
| 5<br><br><br><br>A girl is reading a book about penguins. | 6<br><br><br><br>A boy is writing a report about dolphins. |

Newcomer Program, Grades 3-6 • Prentice Hall Regents   © by Judie Haynes and Elizabeth Claire

# In Science Class – 4

## Complete the crossword puzzle. Use the picture clues below.

| ACROSS | | DOWN | |
|---|---|---|---|

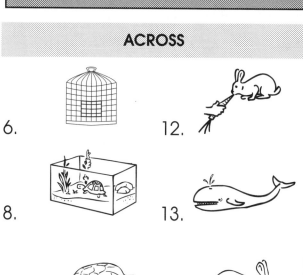

6.      12.

8.      13.

9.      15.

10.

1.      7.

2.      8.

3.      11.

4.      14.

5.

Name _____

Date _____

# In the Computer Room

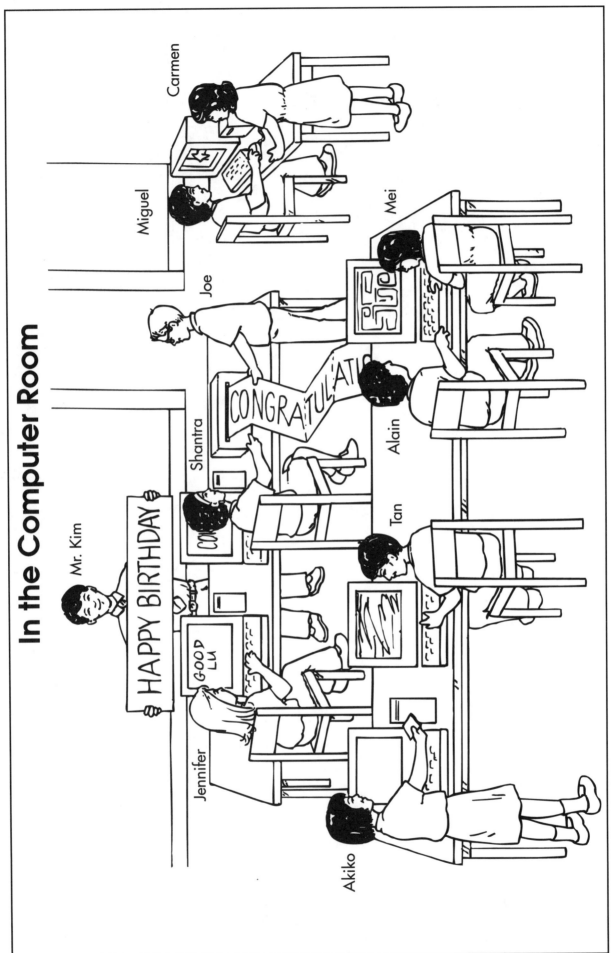

Carmen

Miguel

Joe

Mei

Shantra

Alain

Tan

Mr. Kim

HAPPY BIRTHDAY

CONGRATULATIONS

GOOD LU

Jennifer

Akiko

Instructions: page T57

112

Newcomer Program, Grades 3-6 • Prentice Hall Regents    © by Judie Haynes and Elizabeth Claire

# In the Computer Room – 1

## A. Look, listen, and read.

This is the computer room. The computer teacher's name is Mr. Kim. Mr. Kim is showing the class how to make a banner. Akiko is putting a floppy disk in the disk drive. Jennifer is typing on a keyboard. The printer is printing Shantra's banner. Joe is watching. Miguel is teaching Carmen how to use the mouse. Alain and Mei are playing a computer game. They are looking at the computer screen. Tan's computer doesn't work.

## B. Circle the correct answer.

| | | |
|---|---|---|
| 1. Akiko and Jennifer are playing a computer game. | **Yes** | **No** |
| 2. The teacher's name is Mrs. Kim. | **Yes** | **No** |
| 3. Jennifer is typing on a keyboard. | **Yes** | **No** |
| 4. Mr. Kim is showing the class how to make a banner. | **Yes** | **No** |
| 5. Carmen is teaching Miguel to use the mouse. | **Yes** | **No** |
| 6. Mei is playing a computer game. | **Yes** | **No** |
| 7. The printer is printing Joe's banner. | **Yes** | **No** |
| 8. Shantra is putting a floppy disk in the disk drive. | **Yes** | **No** |
| 9. Tan's computer doesn't work. | **Yes** | **No** |
| 10. Alain is looking at the computer screen. | **Yes** | **No** |

Instructions: page T57

# In the Computer Room – 2

## A. Listen, read, and write.

| printing | mouse | keyboard | floppy disk | screen |
|----------|-------|----------|-------------|--------|
| teaching | room | disk drive | banner | work |

This is the computer _____. The computer

teacher's name is Mr. Kim. Mr. Kim is showing the class how to

make a _____. Akiko is putting a

_____ in the _____. Jennifer

is typing on a _____. The printer is

_____ Shantra's banner. Joe is watching.

Miguel is _____ Carmen how to use the

_____. Akiko and Mei are playing a computer

game. They are looking at the computer _____.

Tan's computer doesn't _____.

## B. Match. Write the letters.

_____ 1. Akiko          a. computer doesn't work.

_____ 2. Tan's          b. is the computer teacher.

_____ 3. Jennifer       c. is typing on a keyboard.

_____ 4. Miguel         d. are playing a computer game.

_____ 5. Mr. Kim        e. is putting a floppy disk in the disk drive.

_____ 6. Alain and      f. is teaching Carmen how to use the
         Mei                mouse.

Newcomer Program, Grades 3-6 • Prentice Hall Regents   © by Judie Haynes and Elizabeth Claire

# In the Computer Room – 3

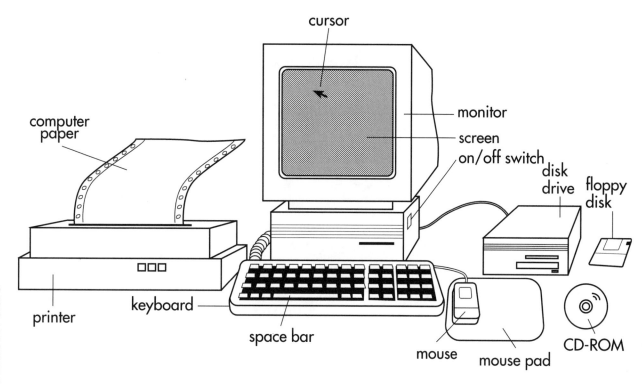

## Use words from the picture to complete the sentences.

1. You type on the _____.

2. You put a _____ _____ in the
   disk drive.

3. You can also put a _____ in the disk drive.

4. The mouse moves the _____ on the screen.

5. The _____ turns off the computer.

6. When you type on the keyboard, you see your work on the
   computer _____.

7. The screen is part of the _____.

8. You can print a banner on the _____.

# In the Computer Room – 4

## Find and circle these words in the puzzle.

| | | | | |
|---|---|---|---|---|
| banner | computer | ~~watching~~ | disk drive | game |
| mouse | keyboard | printing | floppy disk | playing |
| printer | putting | show | teacher | screen |
| looking | work | typing | showing | CD-ROM |

```
(W  A  T  C  H  I  N  G)  G  M  Z  L  K  A  L
 O  I  Z  C  X  B  A  N  N  E  R  G  E  E  O
 R  Y  I  A  U  C  R  K  V  A  F  I  Y  S  O
 K  B  T  B  P  R  I  N  T  I  N  G  B  C  K
 T  E  A  C  H  E  R  Z  F  Z  L  C  O  R  I
 S  S  I  G  A  M  E  C  I  Q  P  O  A  E  N
 X  T  Q  T  Y  P  I  N  G  S  U  M  R  E  G
 I  D  I  S  K  D  R  I  V  E  T  P  D  N  U
 G  X  T  R  W  R  J  B  O  Q  T  U  C  L  R
 A  R  J  M  O  U  S  E  X  V  I  T  Q  X  C
 O  O  H  V  P  S  H  Z  L  Y  N  E  M  U  D
 S  O  H  M  P  L  A  Y  I  N  G  R  B  K  R
 H  M  V  M  U  U  N  S  H  O  W  I  N  G  O
 O  R  F  L  O  P  P  Y  D  I  S  K  O  H  M
 W  L  D  M  Q  P  R  I  N  T  E  R  F  G  B
```

Newcomer Program, Grades 3-6 • Prentice Hall Regents   © by Judie Haynes and Elizabeth Claire

# In the Park

# In the Park – 1

## A. Look, listen, and read.

This is a park. It's a beautiful day. The sun is shining. Akiko and Palo are swinging. Nadia is pushing Palo. Jennifer and Joe are playing catch. Joe is throwing a ball for Jennifer to catch. Miguel is skating. Po Wen fell down. Shantra is climbing a tree. Alain is flying a kite. A woman is sitting on a bench. She is holding her baby. The baby is crying.

## B. Circle the correct answer.

| | | |
|---|---|---|
| 1. It's raining. | Yes | No |
| 2. This is a park. | Yes | No |
| 3. Some children are swinging. | Yes | No |
| 4. A girl is throwing a ball for a boy to catch. | Yes | No |
| 5. Shantra is climbing a bench. | Yes | No |
| 6. Nadia is flying a kite. | Yes | No |
| 7. A woman is sitting on a bench. | Yes | No |
| 8. She is holding a kitten. | Yes | No |
| 9. The baby is happy. | Yes | No |
| 10. Po Wen fell down. | Yes | No |

Newcomer Program, Grades 3–6 • Prentice Hall Regents    © by Judie Haynes and Elizabeth Claire

# In the Park – 2

## A.  Match. Write the letters.

_____ 1.  sun

_____ 2.  kite

_____ 3.  bench

_____ 4.  tree

_____ 5.  roller blades

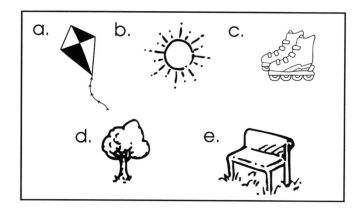

## B. Listen, read, and write.

| crying | sun | sitting | climbing | pushing |
| park | Joe | catch | skating | holding |
| playing | kite | Po Wen | swinging | beautiful |

This is a _____ . It's a _____

day. The _____ is shining. Akiko and Palo are

_____ . Jennifer and Joe are

_____ catch. _____ is

throwing a ball for Jennifer to _____ . Miguel is

_____ . _____ fell down.

Shantra is _____ a tree. Alain is flying a

_____ . A woman is _____

on a bench. She is _____ her baby. The baby

is _____ .

Newcomer Program, Grades 3–6 • Prentice Hall Regents    © by Judie Haynes and Elizabeth Claire

# In the Park – 3

## Draw a picture for each sentence.

| | |
|---|---|
| **1** | **2** |
| A boy and girl are swinging. | A girl is throwing a ball. |
| **3** | **4** |
| A girl is climbing a tree. | Two children are roller-blading. |
| **5** | **6** |
| A girl fell down. | Two boys are flying a kite. |

Newcomer Program, Grades 3-6 • Prentice Hall Regents   © by Judie Haynes and Elizabeth Claire

# Around the Town

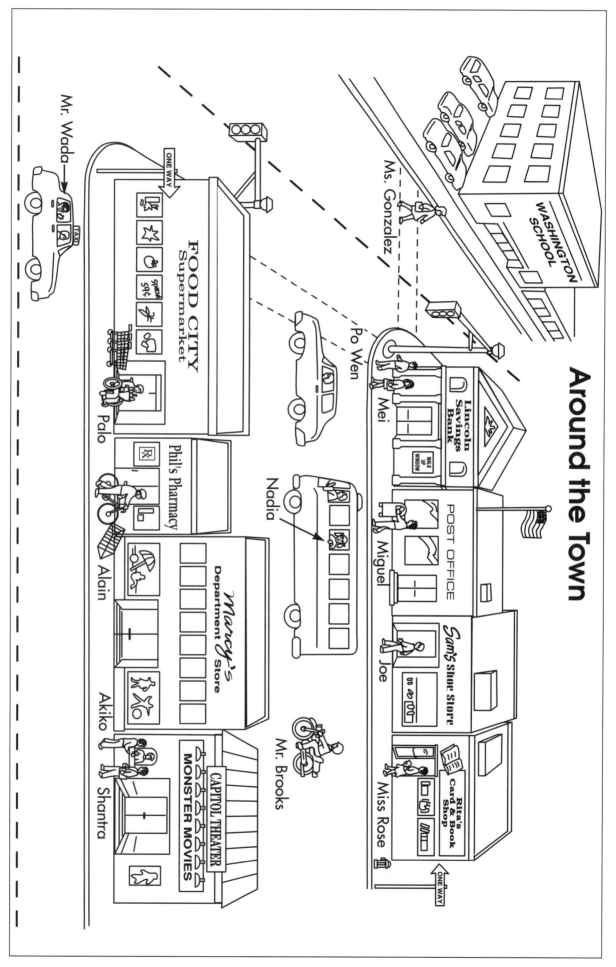

# Around the Town – 1

## A. Look, listen, and read.

There are many people in town today. Mr. Wada is in a taxi. The taxi is going by the supermarket. Nadia is riding on a bus. Mr. Brooks is riding a motorcycle. The motorcycle is behind the bus. Ms. Gonzalez is crossing the street. Po Wen and Mei are at the corner. They are waiting for the traffic light to change. Miguel is in front of the post office. He is mailing a letter. Joe is walking on the sidewalk near the shoe store. Miss Rose is going into the Card and Book Shop. Palo is coming out of the supermarket. He is carrying a bag of groceries. Alain is parking his bicycle in front of the pharmacy. Akiko and Shantra are buying tickets at the theater. They want to see a movie.

## B. Check (✔) the correct answer.

|  | Yes | No |
|---|---|---|
| 1. Mr. Brooks is in a taxi. |  |  |
| 2. Mr. Wada is riding a motorcycle. |  |  |
| 3. Ms. Gonzalez is going to the bank. |  |  |
| 4. Po Wen and Joe are waiting for the traffic light to change. |  |  |
| 5. Alain is mailing a letter. |  |  |
| 6. Joe is coming out of the pharmacy. |  |  |
| 7. Miss Rose is going into the Card and Book Shop. |  |  |
| 8. Palo is going into the supermarket. |  |  |

Newcomer Program, Grades 3-6 • Prentice Hall Regents   © by Judie Haynes and Elizabeth Claire

# Around the Town – 2

## Listen, read, and write.

| | | | | | |
|---|---|---|---|---|---|
| people | motorcycle | sidewalk | town | crossing | riding |
| tickets | supermarket | mailing | taxi | parking | into |
| waiting | in front of | behind | light | bicycle | corner |

There are many _____ in _____

today.  Mr. Wada is in a taxi. The _____ is going by

the supermarket. Nadia is _____ on a bus. Mr.

Brooks is riding a _____. The motorcycle is

_____ the bus. Ms. Gonzalez is

_____ the street. Po Wen and Mei are at

the _____. They are _____ for the

traffic _____ to change. Miguel is

_____ the post office. He is _____ a

letter. Joe is walking on the _____ near the shoe

store. Miss Rose is going _____ the Card and Book

Shop. Palo is coming out of the _____. He is

carrying a bag of groceries. Alain is _____ his

_____ in front of the pharmacy. Akiko and Shantra

are buying _____ at the theater. They want to see

a movie.

Instructions: pages T57, T58

# Around the Town – 3

## A. Match each action with a place.  Write the letters.

_____ 1. mail a letter        a. the department store

_____ 2. buy boots        b. the pharmacy

_____ 3. see a movie        c. the book and card shop

_____ 4. buy Band-Aids        d. the post office

_____ 5. save money        e. the shoe store

_____ 6. shop for groceries        f. the movie theater

_____ 7. buy a new coat        g. the bank

_____ 8. find a birthday card        h. the supermarket

| out of | in front of | near | behind | at | into | beside | on |
|---|---|---|---|---|---|---|---|

## B. Write the correct word in each sentence.

1. Miss Rose is going _____ the Card and Book Shop.

2. The motorcycle is _____ the bus.

3. Nadia is riding _____ the bus.

4. Palo is coming _____ the supermarket.

5. Joe is walking on the sidewalk _____ the shoe store.

6. Miguel is _____ the supermarket.

Newcomer Program, Grades 3-6 • Prentice Hall Regents   © by Judie Haynes and Elizabeth Claire

Name _____ Date _____

# Around the Town – 4

## Label each picture. Write what you can buy there.

1. __milk__ _____
   _____
   _____
   _____
   _____
   _____
   _____

2. __blouse__ _____
   _____
   _____
   _____
   _____
   _____

3. __sandals__ _____
   _____
   _____
   _____
   _____
   _____

Newcomer Program, Grades 3-6 • Prentice Hall Regents © by Judie Haynes and Elizabeth Claire

125　　　　Instructions: pages T57, T59

# Family Picture

**Draw yourself and your family.  Label each person.**

| grandfather | mother | uncle | aunt |
| grandmother | father | cousin | son |
| daughter | brother | sister | |

Newcomer Program, Grades 3–6 • Prentice Hall Regents    © by Judie Haynes and Elizabeth Claire

# Family Fun

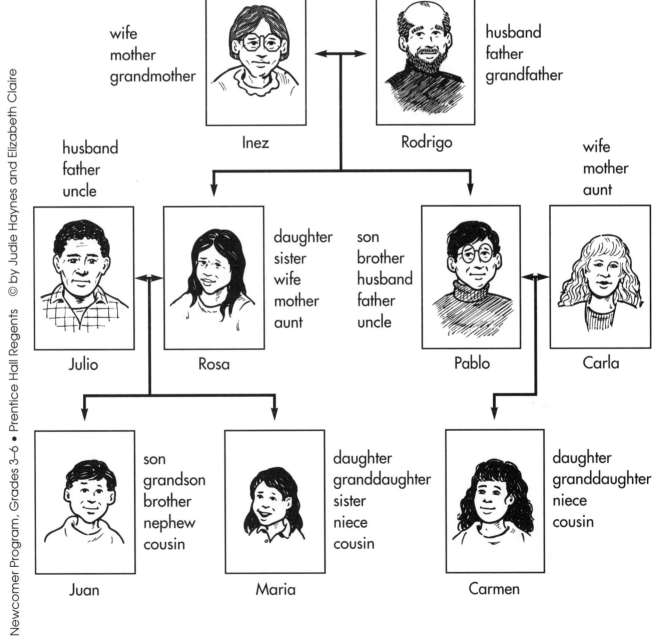

wife
mother
grandmother

Inez

husband
father
grandfather

Rodrigo

husband
father
uncle

Julio

daughter
sister
wife
mother
aunt

Rosa

son
brother
husband
father
uncle

Pablo

wife
mother
aunt

Carla

son
grandson
brother
nephew
cousin

Juan

daughter
granddaughter
sister
niece
cousin

Maria

daughter
granddaughter
niece
cousin

Carmen

# Who Are These People?

Julio    Juan    Inez    Maria    Rosa    Carla    Pablo    Carmen

## Write names to finish the sentences.

1. Juan's **sister** is _____.

2. Maria's **brother** is _____.

3. Rosa's **mother** is _____.

4. Inez's **grandson** is _____.

5. Rosa's **son** is _____.

6. Julio's **daughter** is _____.

7. Carmen's **cousins** are _____ and _____.

8. Maria's **uncle** is _____.

9. Carmen's **grandmother** is _____.

10. Pablo's **wife** is _____.

11. Carla's **husband** is _____.

12. Juan's **aunt** is _____.

13. Julio's **niece** is _____.

14. Carla's **nephew** is _____.

Newcomer Program, Grades 3–6 • Prentice Hall Regents    © by Judie Haynes and Elizabeth Claire

Name _____ Date _____

# Things to Do – 1

## Where do you like to go?  What do you like to do?

1

go shopping

2

play a musical instrument

3

go roller-blading

4
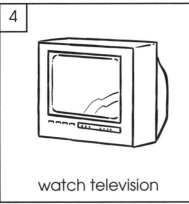
watch television

5

go on a trip

6

go to the beach

7

go to the fair

8

help cook dinner

9
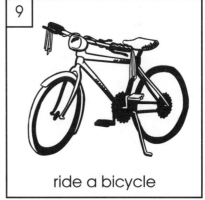
ride a bicycle

10

work on a puzzle

11

play in the snow

12

listen to music

Instructions: page T60

# Things to Do – 2

**Draw things you like to do and places you like to go.
Tell about them.**

Newcomer Program, Grades 3–6 • Prentice Hall Regents    © by Judie Haynes and Elizabeth Claire

Name _____     Date _____

# Safety Signs – 1

## A. What do these signs mean?

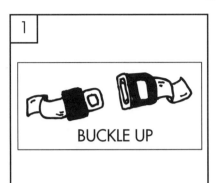

BUCKLE UP

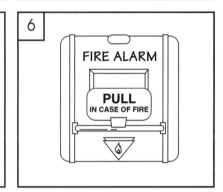

## B. Draw more signs. Tell about them.

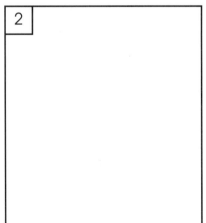

Newcomer Program, Grades 3–6 • Prentice Hall Regents   © by Judie Haynes and Elizabeth Claire

Instructions: page T60

Name _____   Date _____

# Safety Signs – 2

## A. Match. Write the letters.

_____ 1.  Don't eat or drink this.                          a.

_____ 2.  Stop and look before you cross.                  b.

_____ 3.  Always wear a seatbelt.                          c.

_____ 4.  A wheelchair can enter here easily.              d.

_____ 5.  Do not touch. Danger!                            e.

_____ 6.  Cross when it says, "WALK."                      f.

## B. Draw your own safety signs.

| 1 | 2 |
|---|---|
| Say, "NO!" to drugs. | Don't ride with strangers! |

Newcomer Program, Grades 3–6 • Prentice Hall Regents   © by Judie Haynes and Elizabeth Claire

Name _____ Date _____

# The Flag of the United States

## A. Color the flag.

white       blue                                    red       white

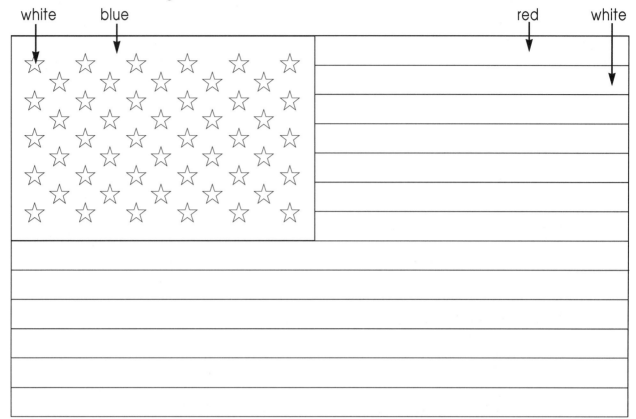

## B. Write the correct numbers. Then answer the questions.

This is the flag of the United States of America. It has _____ stars and _____ stripes. Each star stands for one state. Each stripe stands for one of the original states.

1. How many colors are in the American flag? _____

2. What are the colors in the American flag? _____, _____, and _____.

3. What colors are in the flag of your native country? _____

_____

Name _____ Date _____

# The Pledge of Allegiance

**1**

I pledge allegiance to the flag

**2**
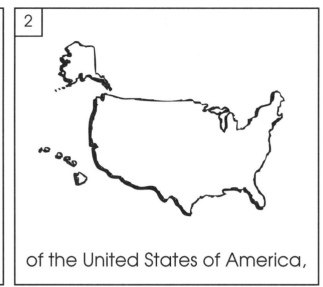
of the United States of America,

**3**
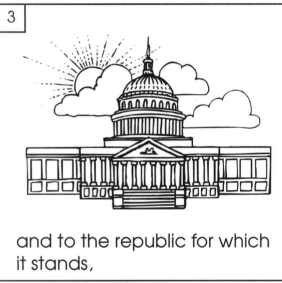
and to the republic for which it stands,

**4**

one nation, under God, indivisible,

**5**

with liberty and justice for all.

Instructions: page T61                    134

Newcomer Program, Grades 3–6 • Prentice Hall Regents   © by Judie Haynes and Elizabeth Claire

# The United States of America – 1

### 1

This is the continent of North America.

The United States is a country in North America.

The United States has two neighbors, Canada and Mexico.

Canada is to the north.

Mexico is to the south.

### 2

The United States touches two oceans.

The Atlantic Ocean is to the east.

The Pacific Ocean is to the west.

The United States also touches the Gulf of Mexico.

The Gulf of Mexico is east of Mexico and south of the United States.

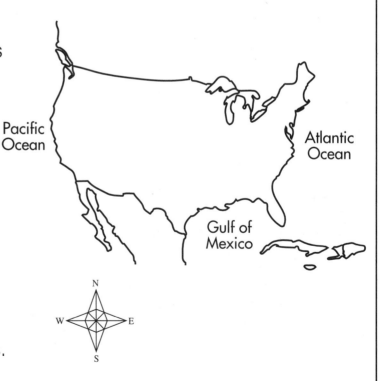

Newcomer Program, Grades 3–6 • Prentice Hall Regents    © by Judie Haynes and Elizabeth Claire

Name _____ Date _____

# The United States of America – 2

**A.** **Find these words in the story on page 135. Underline them. Then write the words in your native language.**

| | | | |
|---|---|---|---|
| neighbors | Mexico | country | south |
| continent | oceans | Pacific | east |
| Canada | United | States | west |
| Atlantic | touches | Gulf | north |

**B.** **Complete the sentences. Use words from above.**

1. North America is a _____.

2. The United States is a _____ in North America.

3. Canada and Mexico are _____ of the United States.

4. _____ is to the north.

5. Mexico is to the _____.

6. The Atlantic Ocean is to the _____.

7. The _____ Ocean is to the _____.

8. The _____ of _____ is east of Mexico and south of the United States.

9. _____ , _____ , and _____ are countries on the continent of North America.

10. _____ and _____ are oceans that touch North America.

Newcomer Program, Grades 3–6 • Prentice Hall Regents    © by Judie Haynes and Elizabeth Claire

# What's the Weather? – 1

| | | |
|---|---|---|
| 1  The sun is shining. It's a sunny day. | 2  It's a cloudy day. | 3  It's partly cloudy. It's partly sunny. |
| 4  It's foggy. | 5  It's raining. | 6  It's pouring. |
| 7  It's snowing. | 8  It's sleeting. | 9  It's hailing. |

Newcomer Program, Grades 3–6 • Prentice Hall Regents    © by Judie Haynes and Elizabeth Claire

Instructions: page T61

Name _____   Date _____

# What's the Weather? – 2

a windy day

a thunderstorm, with lightning

a hurricane

a tornado

a blizzard

smog

flood

drought

Newcomer Program, Grades 3–6 • Prentice Hall Regents     © by Judie Haynes and Elizabeth Claire

Name _____ Date _____

# What's the Temperature?

**Draw a picture for each answer.**

1

It's a hot day.
It is _____ degrees
Fahrenheit. (_____ °F.)

2

It's a cold day.
It is _____ degrees
Fahrenheit. (_____ °F.)

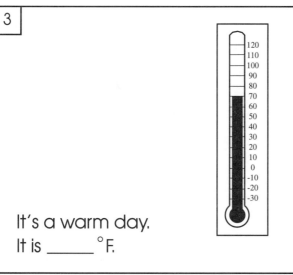

3

It's a warm day.
It is _____ °F.

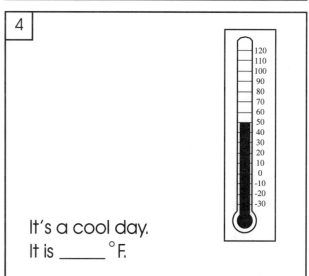

4

It's a cool day.
It is _____ °F.

5

What is the
temperature outside
now? _____

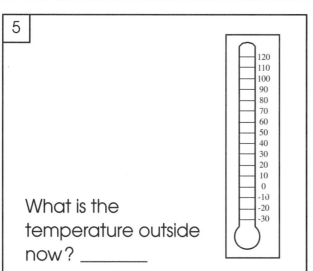

6

What is the
temperature inside?

_____

Newcomer Program, Grades 3–6 • Prentice Hall Regents     © by Judie Haynes and Elizabeth Claire

Instructions: page T62

Name _____ Date _____

# Today's Weather

## A. Check (✔) boxes to show today's weather.

1. Today, it is ❑ hot  and ❑ sunny.

             ❑ warm                    ❑ cloudy.

             ❑ cool                     ❑ partly cloudy.

             ❑ cold 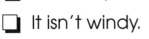      ❑ foggy.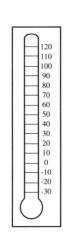

2. ❑ It's windy.
   ❑ It isn't windy.

3. ❑ It's raining.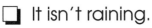
   ❑ It isn't raining.

4. ❑ It's snowing.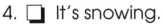
   ❑ It isn't snowing.

5. Today, at _____ , the temperature was _____ °F.
              (time)

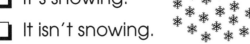

## B. Write about today's weather. Copy the weather report from above.

_____

_____

_____

_____

_____

_____

_____

Newcomer Program, Grades 3–6 • Prentice Hall Regents    © by Judie Haynes and Elizabeth Claire

# Yesterday's Weather

## A. Check (✔) boxes to show yesterday's weather.

1. Yesterday, it was  ☐ hot   and  ☐ sunny.

   ☐ warm  ☐ cloudy.

   ☐ cool  ☐ partly cloudy.

   ☐ cold   ☐ foggy.

2. ☐ It was windy.
   ☐ It wasn't windy.

3. ☐ It rained.
   ☐ It didn't rain.

4. ☐ It snowed.
   ☐ It didn't snow.

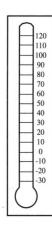

5. Yesterday, at _____ , the temperature
   (time)
   was _____ °F.

## B. Write about yesterday's weather. Copy the weather report from above.

_____

_____

_____

_____

_____

_____

_____

Newcomer Program, Grades 3–6 • Prentice Hall Regents    © by Judie Haynes and Elizabeth Claire

Name _____ Date _____

# Weather Forecast

**A. Check (✔) boxes to show what you think tomorrow's weather will be.**

1. Tomorrow, _____ , it will be
   (date)

   ☐ hot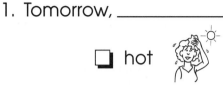

   ☐ warm

   ☐ cool

   ☐ cold

   and ☐ sunny.

   ☐ cloudy.

   ☐ partly cloudy.

   ☐ foggy.

2. ☐ It will be windy.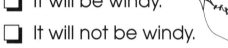
   ☐ It will not be windy.

3. ☐ It will rain.
   ☐ It won't rain.

4. ☐ It will snow.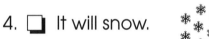
   ☐ It won't snow.

5. Tomorrow morning, at _____ , the temperature
   (time)

   will be _____ °F.

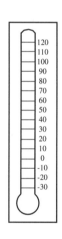

**B. Write about tomorrow's weather. Copy the weather forecast from above.**

_____

_____

_____

_____

_____

Newcomer Program, Grades 3–6 • Prentice Hall Regents   © by Judie Haynes and Elizabeth Claire

# Weather Records – 1

## A. Keep a temperature chart.

1. Read your thermometer at the same time each day.

2. Mark the temperature on page 144.

3. Then connect the marks to make a graph.

## B. Keep a weather calendar.

1. Use page 145.

2. Use these symbols to show the weather each day.

sunny      cloudy      partly cloudy      rain

snow      storm      wind

**Sample Graph**

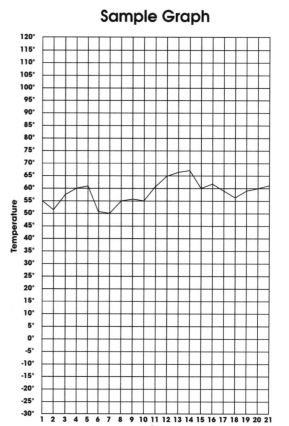

## C. Use your weather records to complete these sentences.

1. The hottest temperature was _____ °F.

2. The coldest temperature was _____ °F.

3. _____ days were sunny.

4. _____ days were cloudy.

5. It rained on _____ days.

6. It snowed on _____ days.

7. It _____ .

8. It _____ .

# Weather Records – 2

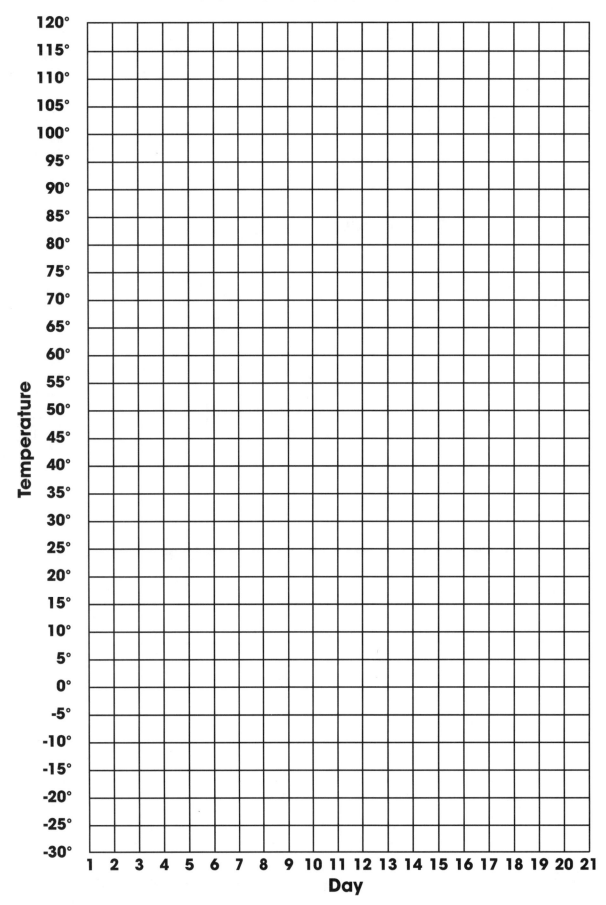

Newcomer Program, Grades 3–6 • Prentice Hall Regents    © by Judie Haynes and Elizabeth Claire

Name _____ Date _____

# Weather Records – 3

| Date | Temperature | Weather |
|------|-------------|---------|
| Sunday _____ | _____ | Today it _____ |
| Monday _____ | _____ | Today it _____ |
| Tuesday _____ | _____ | Today it _____ |
| Wednesday _____ | _____ | Today it _____ |
| Thursday _____ | _____ | Today it _____ |
| Friday _____ | _____ | Today it _____ |
| Saturday _____ | _____ | Today it _____ |

Instructions: page T63

# The Body

## Write the correct word on each line.

| | | | |
|---|---|---|---|
| arm | feet | head | chest |
| back | foot | knee | shoulder |
| neck | hand | leg | stomach |

1. _____

2. _____

3. _____

4. _____

5. _____

6. _____

7. _____

8. _____

9. _____

10. _____

11. _____

12. _____

Newcomer Program, Grades 3–6 • Prentice Hall Regents   © by Judie Haynes and Elizabeth Claire

# The Face

## Write the correct word on each line.

| cheek | ear | forehead | hair |
|-------|-----|----------|------|
| chin | eye | mouth | nose |

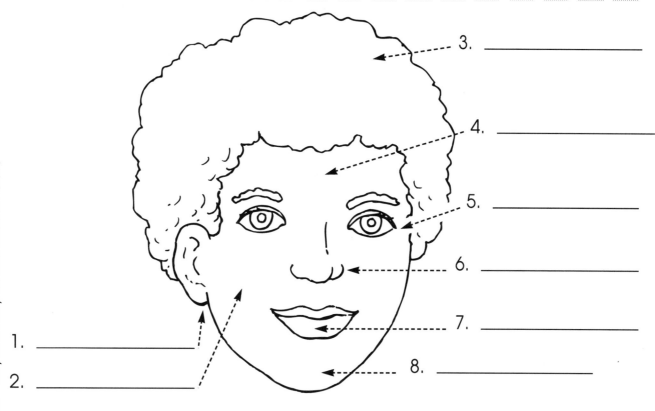

3. _____

4. _____

5. _____

6. _____

7. _____

8. _____

1. _____

2. _____

| eyebrow | eyelid | pupil | tongue | eyelash | lip | teeth |
|---------|--------|-------|--------|---------|-----|-------|

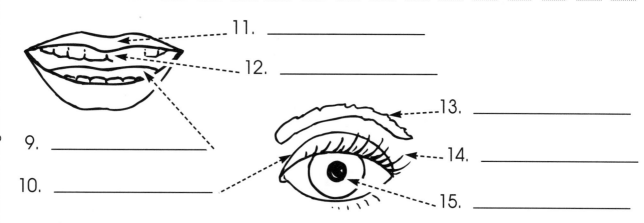

11. _____

12. _____

9. _____

10. _____

13. _____

14. _____

15. _____

Instructions: page T64

# Look in the Mirror

## A. Draw your face.

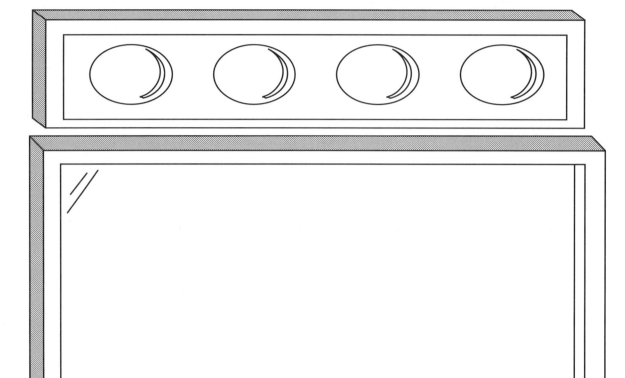

## B. Tell what you see.

My eyes are _____. My hair is _____.

_____

_____

Newcomer Program, Grades 3–6 • Prentice Hall Regents    © by Judie Haynes and Elizabeth Claire

# Find Someone Who . . .

eye          short hair          long hair          curly hair

straight hair          pony tails          black hair          braids

## Write sentences about your classmates.  If you don't know someone's name, ask.

1. Find someone who has brown eyes.

   _____

2. Find someone who has short hair.

   _____

3. Find someone who has braids.

   _____

4. Find someone who has a pony tail.

   _____

5. Find someone who doesn't have black hair.

   _____

6. Find someone who doesn't have curly hair.

   _____

7. Find someone who doesn't have straight hair.

   _____

8. Find someone who doesn't have brown eyes.

   _____

Name _____ Date _____

# What Hurts?

| | |
|---|---|
| 1 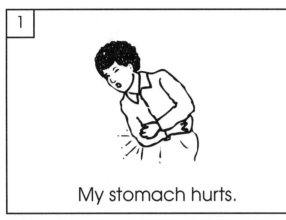 My stomach hurts. | 2 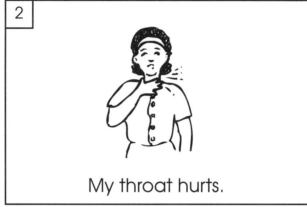 My throat hurts. |
| 3 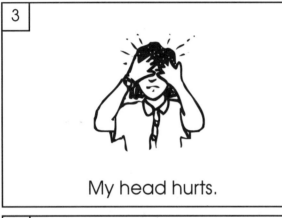 My head hurts. | 4 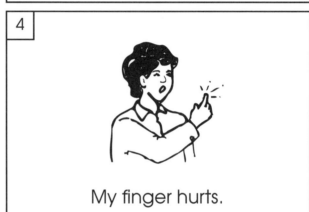 My finger hurts. |
| 5 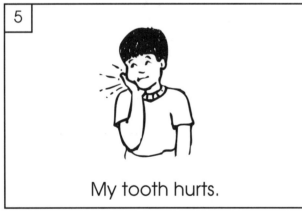 My tooth hurts. | 6  My side hurts. |
| 7 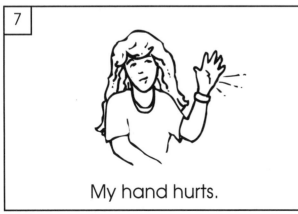 My hand hurts. | 8 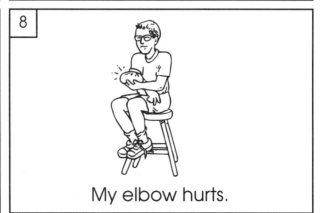 My elbow hurts. |

Newcomer Program, Grades 3–6 • Prentice Hall Regents    © by Judie Haynes and Elizabeth Claire

Name _____ Date _____

# What's the Matter?

## A. How do you feel?

1

I feel fine!

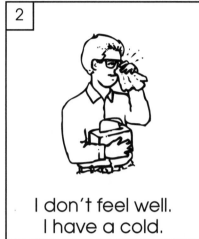

2

I don't feel well.
I have a cold.

3

I'm hurt.
I fell down.

## B. What can you do to feel better?

1

I can visit the nurse.

2

I can rest.

3

I can use an ice pak.

4

I can call home.

## C. Think of a time you didn't feel well.
   Tell what you did to get better.

Instructions: page T65

# Senses – 1

## A. You see with your eyes.   What can you see?

| 1  a picture | 2 _____ |
|---|---|
| 3 _____ | 4 _____ |

## B. You hear with your ears.  What can you hear?

| 1 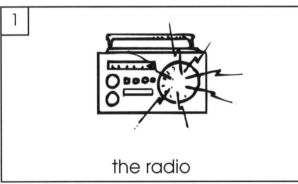 the radio | 2 _____ |
|---|---|
| 3 _____ | 4 _____ |

Newcomer Program, Grades 3–6 • Prentice Hall Regents    © by Judie Haynes and Elizabeth Claire

Name _____ Date _____

# Senses – 2

## A. You smell with your nose.  What can you smell?

| 1   flowers | 2   _____ |
|---|---|
| 3  _____ | 4  _____ |

## B. You taste with your tongue.  What can you taste?

| 1   apples | 2  _____ |
|---|---|
| 3  _____ | 4  _____ |

Instructions: page T66

Name _____  Date _____

# Senses – 3

**A. You touch and feel with your fingers.
What can you feel?**

| hard | rough | hot | sticky |
|------|-------|-----|--------|
| soft | smooth | cold | sharp |

**1**

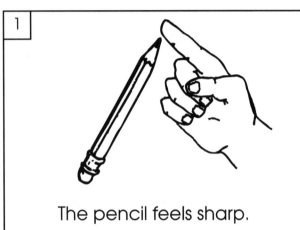

The pencil feels sharp.

**2**

_____

**3**

_____

**4**

_____

**5**

_____

**6**

_____

Newcomer Program, Grades 3–6 • Prentice Hall Regents    © by Judie Haynes and Elizabeth Claire

# Animal Cards – 1

| | | | | |
|---|---|---|---|---|
| monkey | elephant | zebra | seal | lion |
| kangaroo | parrot | tiger | giraffe | cow |
| horse | sheep | duck | chicken | pig |
| cat | dog | squirrel | fox | rabbit |
| snake | mouse | turtle | bear | deer |
| owl | bird | fish | whale | hippopotamus |

CLUCK CLUCK

Instructions: page T66

# Animal Cards – 2

| | | | | |
|---|---|---|---|---|
| fly | bat | frog | moose | panda |
| koala bear | goat | hawk | ostrich | flamingo |
| turkey | lizard | camel | sea otter | iguana |
| beetle | skunk | spider | eagle | seahorse |
| grasshopper | dolphin | polar bear | ant | rhinocerous |
| shark | alligator | octopus | butterfly | bee |

Newcomer Program, Grades 3-6 • Prentice Hall Regents    © by Judie Haynes and Elizabeth Claire

# Animal Body Parts Cards

| | | | |
|---|---|---|---|
| hooves | paws | feet | fins |
| noses | beaks | flippers | wings |
| tails | fur | shells | scales |
| feathers | pouch | stripes | spots |
| horns | antlers | tentacles | antennae |

Instructions: page T66

# Tell About These Animals

**Label the parts of each animal.**

legs   fur   tail
ears   paw  whiskers

beak
claws
tail
wing
feathers

shell   claws
neck   tail
mouth  eye

Newcomer Program, Grades 3–6 • Prentice Hall Regents © by Judie Haynes and Elizabeth Claire

# How Do Animals Move?

**Classify the animals. First use the Animal Cards.**
**Then write the animal names.**

| Fly | Hop/Jump | Walk/Run/Crawl | Swim |
|---|---|---|---|
| | | | |
| | | | |
| | | | |
| | | | |
| | | | |

Newcomer Program, Grades 3–6 • Prentice Hall Regents   © by Judie Haynes and Elizabeth Claire

# What Animals Go Together?

**Classify the animals. First use the Animal Cards.**
**Then write the animal names.**

| Mammals | Birds | Insects and Arachnids |
|---|---|---|
| | | |

| Reptiles | Amphibians | Fish |
|---|---|---|
| | | |

Newcomer Program, Grades 3–6 • Prentice Hall Regents　© by Judie Haynes and Elizabeth Claire

# Animal Homes and Habitats Cards

nest

web

grass

water

tree

underground

forest

desert

grassland

cave

mountains

river

zoo

farm

house

Instructions: page T67

# What Animals Live Here?

Put a habitat card at the top of each column.
Use Animal Cards to show what lives in each place.
Label the columns.  Write the animal names in each one.

| | |
|---|---|
| | |
| | |

Newcomer Program, Grades 3–6 • Prentice Hall Regents   © by Judie Haynes and Elizabeth Claire

# What Do Animals Eat?

**Classify the animals.  First use the Animal Cards.**
**Then write the animal names.**

| Herbivores (eat plants) | Carnivores (eat other animals) | Omnivores (eat plants and animals) |
|---|---|---|
| | | |

Instructions: page T68

# What Animal Is This?

**A. Draw an animal.  Show where it lives and what it eats.**

My animal is _____.

**B. Write about the animal in your picture.**

1. This animal lives _____.

2. It eats _____.

3. It moves by _____.

4. It can _____.

5. It has _____.

6. It _____.

Newcomer Program, Grades 3–6 • Prentice Hall Regents    © by Judie Haynes and Elizabeth Claire

Name _____   Date _____

# Different Ways to Read Numbers

**1**

# 756

seven hundred fifty-six

**2**

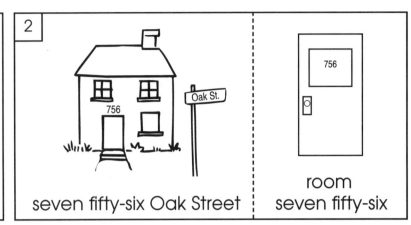

seven fifty-six Oak Street

room
seven fifty-six

**3**

# 1,756

one thousand seven
hundred fifty-six

**4**

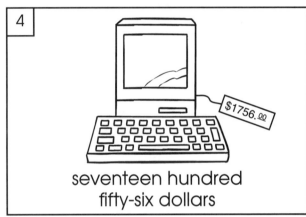

seventeen hundred
fifty-six dollars

**5**

| September 1756 | | | | | | |
|---|---|---|---|---|---|---|
| S | M | T | W | Th | F | S |
|  |  |  |  |  |  |  |
|  |  |  |  |  |  |  |
|  |  |  |  |  |  |  |
|  |  |  |  |  |  |  |

seventeen fifty-six

**6**

201 555-1756

two-oh-one, five-five-five,
one-seven-five-six

## Read these numbers to a classmate.

a. 342

b.
342

c. 1,342

d.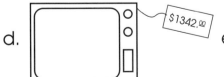
$1342.⁰⁰

e. October 10, 1342

f.
(609) 555-1342

Instructions: page T68

# United States Coins

| Name | Value | Appearance | |
|------|-------|------------|---|
| | | heads | tails |
| penny | one cent<br>1¢ or $.01 | | |
| nickel | five cents<br>5¢ or $.05 | | |
| dime | ten cents<br>10¢ or $.10 | | |
| quarter | twenty-five cents<br>25¢ or $.25 | | |
| half-dollar | fifty cents<br>50¢ or $.50 | | |
| silver dollar | one hundred<br>cents<br>$1.00 | | |

Newcomer Program, Grades 3–6 • Prentice Hall Regents    © by Judie Haynes and Elizabeth Claire

# United States Bills

| Name | Value | Appearance |
|---|---|---|
| one-dollar bill | one hundred cents $1.00 | |
| five-dollar bill | five dollars $5.00 | |
| ten-dollar bill | ten dollars $10.00 | |
| twenty-dollar bill | twenty dollars $20.00 | |
| one hundred-dollar bill | one hundred dollars $100.00 | |

Newcomer Program, Grades 3–6 • Prentice Hall Regents   © by Judie Haynes and Elizabeth Claire

Instructions: page T69

# How Much Is It?

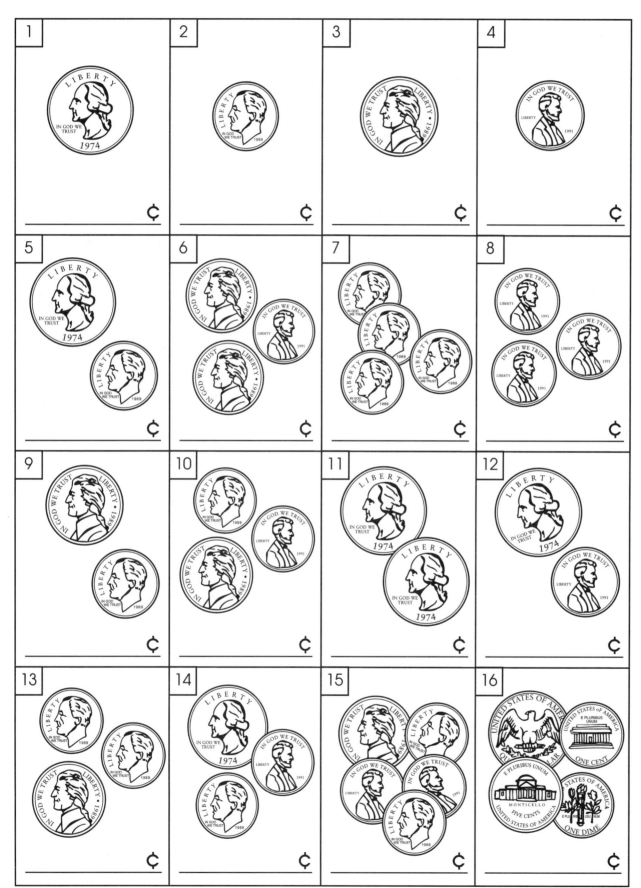

| | | | |
|---|---|---|---|
| 1 ___ ¢ | 2 ___ ¢ | 3 ___ ¢ | 4 ___ ¢ |
| 5 ___ ¢ | 6 ___ ¢ | 7 ___ ¢ | 8 ___ ¢ |
| 9 ___ ¢ | 10 ___ ¢ | 11 ___ ¢ | 12 ___ ¢ |
| 13 ___ ¢ | 14 ___ ¢ | 15 ___ ¢ | 16 ___ ¢ |

# Going Shopping – 1

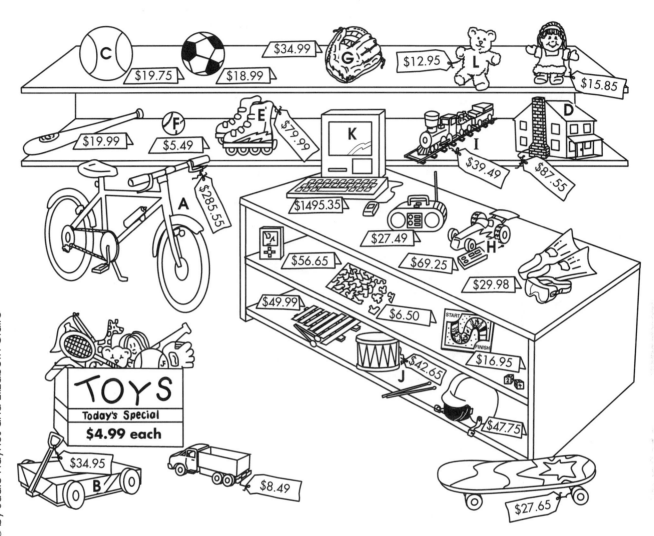

## Find these in the store.  Write what each one costs.

_____ A.  bicycle

_____ B.  wagon

_____ C.  basketball

_____ D.  doll house

_____ E.  roller blades

_____ F.  baseball

_____ G.  baseball mitt

_____ H.  radio-controlled car

_____ I.  model train

_____ J.  drum

_____ K.  computer

_____ L.  bear

# Going Shopping – 2

## A. Use page 169 to answer these questions.

1. Which toy costs the most? _____

2. Which toy costs the least? _____

3. Which toy costs more than the truck and less than the roller blades? _____

4. Which is more expensive, the basketball or the soccer ball?

   _____

5. Which is less expensive, the radio-controlled car or the bicycle?

   _____

## B. Pretend you have $100.00. What can you buy from page 169? Make a list.

1. _____     5. _____

2. _____     6. _____

3. _____     7. _____

4. _____     8. _____

## C. What change will you get from $50.00?

1. You buy a radio for $27.49.

   ____ twenty-dollar bill ____ dollar bills ____ quarters ____ penny

2. You buy a bear for $12.95.

   ____ twenty-dollar bills ____ five-dollar bills ____ dollar bills
   ____ nickel

3. You buy a puzzle and a wagon for $41.45.

   ____ five-dollar bill ____ dollar bills ____ quarters ____ nickel

Newcomer Program, Grades 3–6 • Prentice Hall Regents     © by Judie Haynes and Elizabeth Claire

# Shapes

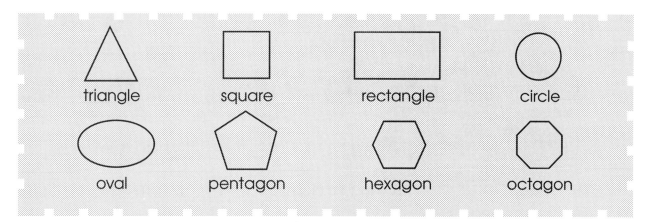

triangle     square     rectangle     circle

oval     pentagon     hexagon     octagon

## A. Draw and label something that has each shape.

| 1 | octagon | 2 | triangle | 3 | oval |

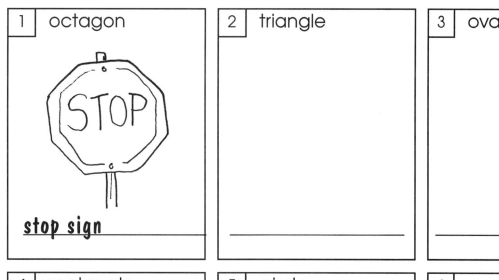

**stop sign** _____

| | | | | | |

| 4 | rectangle | 5 | circle | 6 | square |

_____ _____ _____

## B. Draw a picture on the back of this page. Use all the shapes, if you can. Then label each shape.

# Solid Shapes

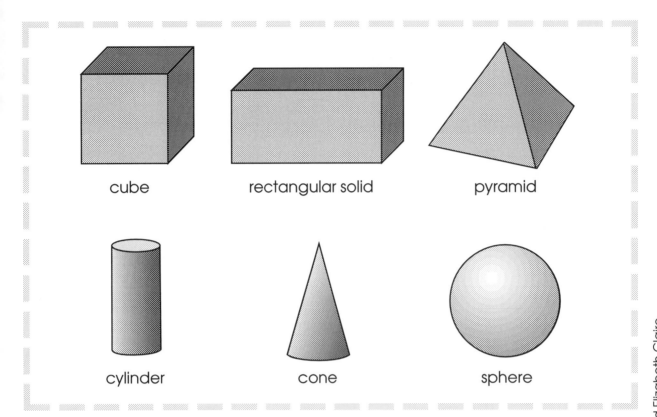

cube          rectangular solid          pyramid

cylinder          cone          sphere

## A. Match. Write the letters.

_____ 1. cone

_____ 2. sphere

_____ 3. cube

_____ 4. pyramid

_____ 5. cylinder

_____ 6. rectangular solid

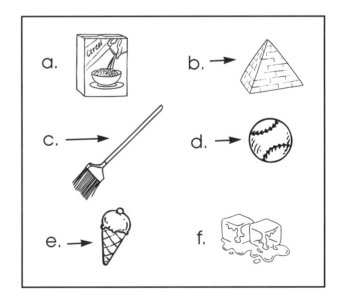

## B. Draw a picture on the back of this page. Use all of the solid shapes, if you can. Label each shape.

Newcomer Program, Grades 3–6 • Prentice Hall Regents    © by Judie Haynes and Elizabeth Claire

# Lines

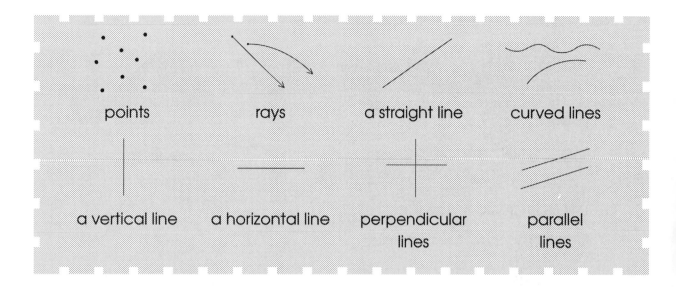

points          rays          a straight line          curved lines

a vertical line          a horizontal line          perpendicular lines          parallel lines

## Draw the lines.

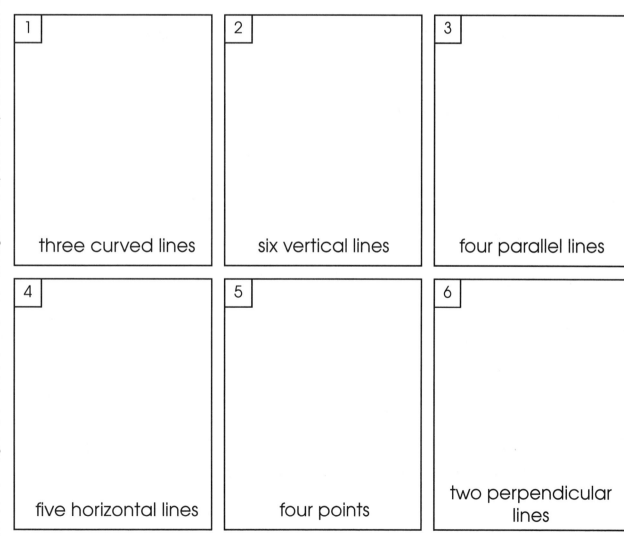

| 1 | 2 | 3 |
|---|---|---|
| three curved lines | six vertical lines | four parallel lines |

| 4 | 5 | 6 |
|---|---|---|
| five horizontal lines | four points | two perpendicular lines |

Name _____ Date _____

# Measure in Inches

## A. Work with a ruler.  One foot is twelve inches.

1. This is one inch.  Mark another inch.

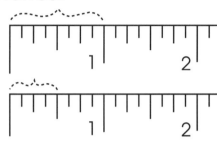

2. This is a half ($\frac{1}{2}$) inch.

   Mark another half inch.

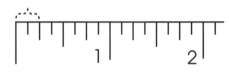

3. This is a quarter ($\frac{1}{4}$) inch.

   Mark another quarter inch.

4. This is an eighth ($\frac{1}{8}$) inch.

   Mark another eighth inch.

5. This is five-eighths ($\frac{5}{8}$) of an inch.

   Mark another five-eighths of an inch.

6. This is three quarters ($\frac{3}{4}$) of an inch.

   Mark another three-quarters of an inch.

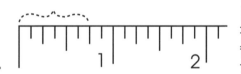

## B. Measure these lines.

1. This line is _____ inches long.    ————————————————

2. This line is _____ inches long.    ——————————————

3. This line is _____ inches long.    ———————————

4. This line is _____ inches long.    ——————————————————

5. This line is _____ inches long.    ————————————————————

## C. Measure things on your desk.

1. My pencil is _____ inches long.

2. This paper is _____ inches long and _____ inches wide.

Newcomer Program, Grades 3–6 • Prentice Hall Regents    © by Judie Haynes and Elizabeth Claire

# Measure Heights

## How tall are the people in the picture?

1. Joe is __5__ feet tall.

2. Mei is _____ feet tall.

3. Mr. Wada is _____ _____ _____.

4. Miss Rose is __5__ __feet__ , __6 inches__ tall.

5. Akiko is _____ _____ , _____ _____ tall.

6. Carmen _____.

7. Mr. Nichols _____.

# Measure Yourself

## Measure yourself with a tape measure.  Finish the sentences.

1. I am _____ feet _____ inches tall.

2. My arm is _____ feet _____ inches long.

3. My leg is _____ feet _____ inches long.

4. My foot is _____ inches long.

5. My head is _____ inches around.

6. My neck is _____ inches around.

7. My waist is _____ inches around.

8. My ankle is _____ inches around.

9. My arm span is _____ feet _____ inches.

10. My longest step is _____ feet _____ inches.

11. My leg is _____ inches longer than my _____.

12. My waist is _____ inches bigger than my _____.

Newcomer Program, Grades 3–6 • Prentice Hall Regents   © by Judie Haynes and Elizabeth Claire